Powerful
Mindset

Powerful Mindset

Memory

Practical Mental Influence

William Walker Atkinson

MEDIA

Published 2019 by Gildan Media LLC
aka G&D Media
www.GandDmedia.com

Front cover design by David Rheinhardt of Pyrographx

Interior design by Meghan Day Healey of Story Horse, LLC

Library of Congress Cataloging-in-Publication Data is available upon request

ISBN: 978-1-7225-0284-3

10 9 8 7 6 5 4 3 2 1

Contents

Introduction

How much control do we have over our life. Are our thoughts and acts based on fate? On the circumstances of our birth? On our environment? Or do we control our own thoughts, our own destinies?

Several deep thinkers in the late nineteenth and early twentieth century studied this phenomenon and preached, wrote and practiced a new way of looking at life. By combining a metaphysical, spiritual and pragmatic approach to the way we think and live, they uncovered the secret of attaining what we truly desire. They called this philosophy by various names such as "New Thought" and "New Civilization."

This philosophy is based on the concept that the human soul is linked with the universal law of supply and we have the power to use it to enrich our lives. To achieve our goals, we must work for it, and in doing this, we may suffer the pains and heartaches of humankind. However, we can do all these things only if we believe in our personal power.

Just as science has shown us we can learn to use the invisible airwaves in radio, television and cell phones, modern philosophers and psychologists are working with unseen natural laws, bringing the human mind out into newfound expressions of conscious power.

Nothing was ever in any human being that is not in you; no one ever had more spiritual or mental power than you can attain, or did greater things than you can accomplish.

The New Thought concept can be summed up in these words:

You can become what you want to be.

All that we achieve and all that we fail to achieve is the direct result of our own thoughts. As we think, so we are; as we continue to think, so we remain. All achievements, whether in the business, intellectual or spiritual world are the result of definitely directed thought, are governed by the same law and are of the same method; the only difference lies in the object of attainment. Those who would accomplish little must sacrifice little; those who would achieve must sacrifice much; those who would attain a great deal must sacrifice a great deal.

William W. Atkinson (1862–1932) was one of the leaders of the New Thought movement. In his early career he practiced law in Pennsylvania, but the stress of this work led to a complete physical and mental breakdown, and financial disaster. He looked for healing and in the late 1880's he found it in the New Thought movement. This resulted in the restoration of his health, mental vigor and material prosperity.

In 1900 he became associate editor of *Suggestion,* a New Thought journal, and wrote his first book, *Thought-Force in Business and Everyday Life,* which covered the powers of personal magnetism, psychic influence, thought-force, concentration, will-power and practical mental science.

Later he became editor of *New Thought* magazine, and wrote many articles covering the precepts of the movement and wrote a great many books on New Thought, which achieved wide circulation. William Walker Atkinson was one of the truly greats of The New Thought Movement.

The two books in this volume are good examples of how Atkinson applied the principles of the New Thought movement to the improvement of memory and the projection of thought from one person to another.

Read these books carefully and absorb the concepts into your mind. However, that alone will not improve your memory or enable you to project your thoughts to others and protect yourself from those who wish to dominate you. To attain these skills, you must practice the recommended techniques every day until they become an integral part of your mentality.

BOOK I

Memory

How to Develop, Train and Use It

CONTENTS

Contents

PREFACE

In your study for the cultivation of the memory, along the lines laid down in this book, the first chapter will inform you thoroughly regarding the importance of the memory to the individual, and what a large part it plays in the entire work of the mind. In the second chapter you will learn the fundamentals of memory retention. Then in the third chapter you will become acquainted with the possibilities of cultivating the memory to a high degree, as evidenced by the instances related of the extreme case of development. The next chapters will discuss memory systems, and prove to you that the only true method is the natural method, which requires work, patience and practice—then make up your mind that you will follow this plan as far as it will take you. Then you will learn the secret of memory—the subconscious region of the mind, in which the records of memory are kept, stored away and indexed, and in which your internal computers are busily at work. This will give you the key to the method. In the following two chapters on attention, and association, you will learn how to apply these important principles. This will be followed by a chapter on the phases of memory, and show you how to take mental stock of yourself, determining in which phase of memory you are strongest, and in which you need development. The next chapters will concentrate on training the eye and ear, and on the training of the special phases of the memory. In the concluding chapter, you will find some general advice and parting instruction.

Once you have read the entire book, return to the chapters dealing with the particular phases of memory in which you have decided to develop yourself, studying the details of the instruction carefully until you know every point of it.

Then, most important of all: *get to work.* The rest is a matter of practice, practice, practice, and rehearsal. Go back to the chapters from time to time, and refresh your mind regarding the details. Re-read each chapter at intervals. Make the book your own, in every sense of the word, by absorbing its contents.

CHAPTER 1

MEMORY: ITS IMPORTANCE

It needs very little argument to convince the average thinking person of the great importance of memory. Even then very few begin to realize just how important is the function of the mind that has to do with the retention of mental impressions. The first thought of the average person when asked to consider the importance of memory is its use in the affairs of every-day life, along developed and cultivated lines, as contrasted with the lesser degrees of its development. In short, one generally thinks of memory in its phase of "a good memory" as contrasted with the opposite phase of "a poor memory." But there is a much broader and fuller meaning of the term than that of even this important phase.

It is true that our success in our every-day business, profession, trade or other occupation depends very materially upon the possession of a good memory. Our value in any walk in life depends to a great extent upon the degree of memory we may have developed. Our memory of faces, names, facts, events, circumstances and other things concerning our every-day work is the measure of our ability to accomplish our tasks. And in the social intercourse of men and women, the possession of a retentive memory, well stocked with available facts, renders its possessor a desirable member of society. And in the higher activities of thought, the memory comes as an invaluable aid to us in marshalling the bits and sections of knowledge we may have acquired, and passing them in review before our cognitive faculties —thus does the soul review its mental possessions.

Memory is more than "a good memory"—it is the means whereby we perform the largest share of our mental work. All knowledge is but remembrance. Memory is a primary and fundamental faculty, without which none other can work: the cement, the bitumen, the matrix in which the other faculties are embedded. Without it all life and thought were an unrelated succession. There is no faculty of the mind that can bring its energy into effect unless the memory is stored with ideas for it to look upon. Memory is the cabinet of imagination, the treasury of reason, the registry of conscience, and the council chamber of thought. Immanuel Kant, the great German philosopher, pronounced memory to be "the most wonderful of the faculties."

Unless the mind possessed the power of treasuring up and recalling its past experiences, no knowledge of any kind could be acquired. If every sensation, thought, or emotion passed entirely from the mind the moment it ceased to be present, then it would be as if it had not been; and it could not be recognized or named should it happen to return.

Such a one would not only be without knowledge—without experience gathered from the past—but also without purpose, aim, or plan regarding the future, for these imply knowledge and require memory. Even voluntary motion, or motion for a purpose, could have no existence without memory, for memory is involved in every purpose. Not only the learning of the scholar, but the inspiration of the poet, the genius of the painter, the heroism of the warrior, all depend upon memory. Even consciousness itself could have no existence without memory for every act of consciousness involves a change from a past state to a present, and did the past state vanish the moment it was past, there could be no consciousness of change. Memory, therefore, may be said to be involved in all conscious existence—a property of every conscious being!

In the building of character and individuality, the memory plays an important part, for upon the strength of the impressions received, and the firmness with which they are retained, depends the fiber of character and individuality. Our experiences are indeed the stepping-stones to greater attainments and at the same time our guides and protectors from danger. If the memory serves us well in this respect we are saved the pain of repeating the mistakes of the past, and may also profit by remembering and thus avoiding the mistakes of others. When memory is preternaturally defective, experience and knowledge will be deficient in proportion, and imprudent conduct and absurd opinion are the necessary consequence. A character retaining a feeble hold of bitter experience, or genuine delight, and unable to revive afterwards the impression of the time is in reality the victim of an intellectual weakness under the guise of a moral weakness. To have constantly before us an estimate of the things that affect us, true to the reality, is one precious condition for having our will always stimulated with an accurate reference to our happiness. Thoroughly educated people, in this respect can carry with them at all times the exact estimate of what they have enjoyed or suffered from every object that has ever affected them, and in case of encounter can present to the enemy as strong a front as if they were under the genuine impression. A full and accurate memory, for pleasure or for pain, is the intellectual basis both of prudence as regards self, and sympathy as regards others.

So we see that the cultivation of the memory is far more than the cultivation and development of a single mental faculty— it is the cultivation and development of our entire mental being—the development of our *selves*.

To many persons the words memory, recollection, and remembrance, have the same meaning, but there is a great difference in the exact shade of meaning of each term. The student of this book should make the distinction between the terms, for by so doing you will be better able to grasp the various points of advice and instruction discussed. Let us examine these terms.

John Locke, the eighteenth century English philosopher, in his celebrated work, the "Essay Concerning Human Understanding" has clearly stated the difference between the meaning of these several terms. He says: "Memory is the power to revive again in our minds those ideas which after imprinting, have disappeared, or have been laid aside out of sight—when an idea again recurs without the operation of the like object on the external sensory, it is *remembrance;* if it be sought after by the mind, and with pain and endeavor found, and brought again into view, *it is recollection."*

In other words, *memory is the power of reproducing in the mind former impressions, or percepts. Remembrance and Recollection are the exercise of that power, the former being involuntary or spontaneous, the latter volitional.* We remember because we cannot help it but we recollect only through positive effort. The act of remembering, taken by itself, is involuntary. In other words, when the mind remembers without having tried to remember, it acts spontaneously. In the narrow, contrasted senses of the two terms, we remember by chance, but recollect by intention, and if the endeavor is successful that which is reproduced becomes, by the very effort to bring it forth, more firmly entrenched in the mind than ever.

The New Psychology makes a little different distinction from that of Locke, as given above. It uses the word memory not only in his sense of "The power to revive, etc.," but also in the sense of the activities of the mind which tend to receive and store away the various impressions of the senses, and the ideas conceived by the mind, to the end that they may be reproduced voluntarily, or involuntarily, thereafter. The distinction between remembrance and recollection, as made by Locke, is adopted as correct by The New Psychology.

It has long been recognized that the memory, in all of its phases, is capable of development, culture, training and guidance through intelligent exercise. Like any other faculty of mind, or physical part, muscle or limb, it may be improved and strengthened. But until recent years, the entire efforts of these memory-developers were directed to the strengthening of that phase of the memory known as "recollection," which, you will remember, Locke defined as an idea or impression "sought after by the mind, and with pain and endeavor found, and brought again into view." The New Psychology goes much further than this. While pointing out the most improved and scientific methods for "recollecting" the impressions and ideas of the memory, it also instructs the student in the use of the proper methods whereby the memory may be stored with clear and distinct impressions which will, thereafter, flow naturally and involuntarily into the field of consciousness when the mind is *thinking* upon the associated subject or line of thought; and which may also be "recollected" by a voluntary effort with far less expenditure of energy than under the old methods and systems.

You will see this idea carried out in detail, as we progress with the various stages of the subject, in this book. You will see that the first thing to do it *to find something to remember;* then to impress that thing clearly and distinctly upon the receptive tablets of the memory; then to exercise the remembrance in the direction of bringing out the stored-away facts of the memory; then to acquire the scientific methods of recollecting special items of memory that may be necessary at some special time. This is the natural method in memory cultivation, as opposed to the artificial systems. It is not only development of the memory, but also development of the mind itself in several of its regions and phases of activity. It is not merely a method of recollecting, but also a method of correct seeing, thinking and remembering. This method recognizes the truth of the verse of the poet, Alexander Pope, who said: "Remembrance and reflection how allied! What thin partitions sense from thought divide!"

Key Points

Memory is the power to revive again in our minds those ideas that after imprinting, have disappeared, or have been laid aside out of sight.

Remembrance is when an idea again recurs without any special effort on our part.

Recollection is when the matter sought after by the mind can only be brought again into *view* with pain and endeavor.

Until recent years, the entire efforts of memory-developers were directed to the strengthening of that phase of the memory known as "recollection"—ideas or impressions "sought after by the mind, and with pain and endeavor found, and brought again into view." The New Psychology goes much further than this. It instructs the student how the memory may be stored with clear and distinct impressions which will, thereafter, flow naturally and involuntarily into the field of consciousness when the mind is *thinking* upon the associated subject or line of thought; and which may also be "recollected" by a voluntary effort with far less expenditure of energy than under the old methods and systems.

CHAPTER 2
CULTIVATION OF THE MEMORY

This book is written with the fundamental intention and idea of pointing out a rational and workable method whereby the memory may be developed, trained and cultivated. Many persons seem to be under the impression that memories are bestowed by nature, in a fixed degree or possibilities, and that little more can be done for them—in short, that memories are born, not made. But the fallacy of any such idea is demonstrated by the investigations and experiments of all the leading authorities, as well as by the results obtained by persons who have developed and cultivated their own memories by individual effort without the assistance of an instructor. But all such improvement, to be real, must be along certain natural lines and in accordance with the well-established laws of psychology, instead of along artificial lines and in defiance of psychological principles. Cultivation of the memory is a far different thing from "trick memory," or feats of mental legerdemain.

That the memory is capable of indefinite improvement, there can be no manner of doubt; but the means of achieving this is not easily defined. The natural as opposed to the artificial memory depends on the relations of sense and the relations of thought—the spontaneous memory of the eye and the ear availing itself of the obvious conjunctions of objects which are furnished by space and time, and the rational memory of those higher combinations which the rational faculties induce upon those lower. The artificial memory proposes to substitute for the natural and necessary relations under which all objects must present and arrange themselves, an entirely new set of relations that are purely arbitrary and mechanical, which excite little or no other interest than that they are to aid us in remembering. It follows that if the mind tasks itself to the special effort of considering objects under these artificial relations, it will give less attention to those which have a direct and legitimate interest for itself. The defects of most methods which have been devised and employed for improving the memory, lie in the fact that while they serve to impress particular subjects on the mind, they do not render the memory, as a whole, ready or attentive. The art of memory may be made more destructive to natural memory than spectacles are to eyes. Most experts agree that natural systems of memory improvement are far more effective than artificial "gimmicks."

Natural systems of memory culture are based upon the fundamental conception that the extent of the memory depends, first, on the daily use we make of it; secondly, upon the attention with which we consider the objects we would impress upon it, and, thirdly, upon the order in which we range our ideas. In sum, the three essentials in the cultivation of the memory are:

Use and exercise; review and practice;

Attention and Interest; and

Intelligent Association.

You will find that in the several chapters of this book dealing with the various phases of memory, first, last, and all the time, the importance of the use and employment of the memory, in the way of employment, exercise, practice and review work is emphasized.

Like any other mental faculty, or physical function, the memory will tend to atrophy by disuse and increase, strengthen and develop by rational exercise and employment within the bounds of moderation. You develop a muscle by exercise; you train any special faculty of the mind in the same way; and you must pursue the same method in the case of the memory, if you would develop it.

Nature's laws are constant, and bear a close analogy to each other. You will also notice the great stress that is placed upon the use of the faculty of attention, accompanied by interest. By attention you acquire the impressions that you file away in your mental record-file of memory; and the degree of attention regulates the depth, clearness and strength of the impression. Without a good record, you cannot expect to obtain a good reproduction of it. Poor recording results in poor reproduction, and the rule applies in the case of the memory as well. You will also notice this when the laws of association, and the principles which govern the subject are explained, as well as when describing the methods whereby the proper associations may be made. Every association that you weld to an idea or an impression serves as a cross-reference in the index, whereby the thing is found by remembrance or recollection when it is needed. One's entire education depends for its efficiency upon this law of association. It is a most important feature in the rational cultivation of the memory, while at the same time being the bane of the artificial systems. Natural associations educate, while artificial ones tend to weaken the powers of the mind, if carried to any great length.

There is no royal road to Memory. The cultivation of the memory depends upon the practice along certain scientific lines according to well established psychological laws. Those who hope for a sure "short cut" will be disappointed, for none such exists. The student ought not to be disappointed to find that memory is no exception to the rule of improvement by proper methodical and long continued exercise. There is no royal road, no short cut, to the improvement of either mind or muscle. But those who follow the rules which psychology has established may know that they are walking in the shortest path, and not wandering aimlessly about. Using these rules, you will advance much faster than those without chart, compass, or pilot. You will find mnemonics of extremely limited use. Improvement comes by orderly steps. Methods that dazzle at first sight never give solid results.

You are urged to pay attention to what is said in other chapters of the book upon the subjects of attention and association. It is not necessary to state here the particulars that are mentioned there. The cultivation of the attention is a prerequisite for good memory, and deficiency in this respect means deficiency not only in the field of memory but also in the general field of mental work.

In all branches of The New Psychology there is found a constant repetition of the injunction to cultivate the faculty of attention and concentration. Haziness of perception lies at the root of many a bad memory. If perception is definite, the first step has been taken toward insuring a good memory. If the first impression is vivid, its effect upon the brain cells is more lasting. All persons ought to practice their visualizing power. This will react upon perception and make it more definite. Visualizing will also form a brain habit of remembering things pictorially, and hence more exactly.

The subject of association must also receive its proper share of attention, for it is by means of association that the stored away records of the memory may be recovered or recollected. Nothing helps the mind so much as order and classification. Classes are few, individuals many: to know the class well is to know what is most essential in the character of the individual, and what burdens the memory least to retain whenever we can discover any relation between facts, it is far easier to remember them. The intelligent law of memory may be summed up in these words: *Endeavor to link by some thought relation each new mental acquisition to an old one.* Bind new facts to other facts by relations of similarity, cause and effect, whole and part, or by any logical relation, and we shall find that when an idea occurs to us, a host of related ideas will flow into the mind. If we wish to prepare a speech or write an article on any subject, pertinent illustrations will suggest themselves. The person whose memory is merely contiguous will wonder how we think of them.

Key Points

Natural systems of memory culture are based upon the fundamental conception extent of the memory depends, first, on the daily use we make of it; secondly, upon the attention with which we consider the objects we would impress upon it, and, thirdly, upon the order in which we range our ideas

In sum, the three essentials in the cultivation of the memory are: (1) Use and exercise; review and practice; (2) Attention and Interest; and (3) Intelligent Association.

The cultivation of the memory depends upon the practice along certain scientific lines according to well established psychological laws. Those who hope for a sure "short cut" will be disappointed, for none such exists. The student ought not to be disappointed to find that memory is no exception to the rule of improvement by proper methodical and long continued exercise. There is no royal road, no short cut, to the improvement of either mind or muscle. But those who follow the rules which psychology has established may know that they are walking in the shortest path, and not wandering aimlessly about.

CHAPTER 3
CELEBRATED CASES OF MEMORY

In order that you may appreciate the marvelous extent of development possible to the memory, here are some examples of mention a number of celebrated cases, past and present. These are exceptional and not necessary in every-day life. They are presented merely to show to what wonderful extent development along these lines is possible.

In India, in the past, the sacred books were committed to memory, and handed down from teacher to student, for ages. And even today it is no uncommon thing for the student to be able to repeat, word for word, some voluminous religious work equal in extent to the New Testament. For examples, the entire text and glossary of Panini's Sanskrit grammar, equal in extent to the entire Bible, were handed down orally for several centuries before being committed to writing. There are Brahmins today who have committed to memory, and who can repeat at will, the entire collection of religious poems known as the *Mahabarata,* consisting of over 300,000 *slokas* or verses. There have been minstrels from ancient times until the present day who have learned by heart with remarkable accuracy immensely long epic poems. This has also been found among Algonquin Indians whose sagas or mythic legends are interminable, and yet are committed word by word accurately. Many people have memorized all or parts of the Bible and can repeat from memory any verse or chapter called for in the whole Scripture.

It is related that Mithridates, the ancient warrior-king, knew the name of every soldier in his great army, and conversed fluently in twenty-two dialects. Pliny relates that Charmides could repeat the contents of every book in his large library. Hortensius, the Roman orator, had a remarkable memory that enabled him to retain and recollect the exact words of his opponent's argument, without making a single notation. On a wager, he attended a great auction sale, which lasted over an entire day, and then called off in their proper order every object sold, the name of its purchaser, and the price thereof. Seneca is said to have acquired the ability to memorize several thousand proper names, and to repeat them in the order in which they had been given him, and also to reverse the order and call off the list backward. He also accomplished the feat of listening to several hundred persons, each of whom gave him a verse; memorizing the same as they proceeded; and then repeating them word for word in the exact order of their delivery—and then reversing the process, with complete success. It is said that the Hebrew Scriptures were saved by the Hebrew priest, Edras, for when the Chaldeans destroyed the manuscripts

Esdras was able to repeat them, word by word to the scribes, who then reproduced them, Some Muslim scholars are able to repeat the entire text of the Koran, letter perfect. Ben Jonson, the English poet, is said to have been able to repeat all of his own works from memory, with the greatest ease.

Great memory was not limited to famous people. Fedosova, a Russian peasant, could repeat over 25,000 poems, folk-songs, legends, fairy-tales, war stories, etc., when she was over seventy years of age. The celebrated "Blind Glick," an aged Scottish beggar, could repeat any verse in the Bible called for, as well as the entire text of all the chapters and books. In modern times, the newspaper contained the accounts of a man named Clark who lived in New York City. He is said to have been able to give the exact presidential vote in each State of the Union since the first election. He could give the population in every town of any size in the world either present or in the past providing there was a record of the same. He could quote from Shakespeare for hours at a time beginning at any given point in any play. He could recite the entire text of the Iliad in the original Greek.

All students of memory know the historical case of the unnamed Dutchman, who is said to have been able to take up a fresh newspaper; to read it all through, including the advertisement; and then to repeat its contents, word for word, from beginning to end. On one occasion he is said to have heaped wonder upon wonder, by repeating the contents of the paper backward, beginning with the last word and ending with the first. An English actor is said to have duplicated this feat, using a large London paper and including the market quotations, reports of the debates in

Parliament, the railroad timetables and the advertisements. A London waiter is said to have performed a similar feat, on a wager, by memorizing and correctly repeating the contents of an eight-page paper. One of the most remarkable instances of extraordinary memory known to history is that of the child Christian Meinecken. When less than four years of age he could repeat the entire Bible; two hundred hymns; five thousand Latin words; and much ecclesiastical history, theory, dogmas, arguments; and an encyclopedic quantity of theological literature. He is said to have practically retained every word that was read to him. His case was abnormal, and he died at an early age.

John Stuart Mill, the British economist, is said to have acquired at the age of three years a fair knowledge of Greek, and to have memorized Hume, Gibbon, and other historians, at the age of eight. Shortly after he mastered and memorized Herodotus, Xenophon, some of Socrates, and six of Plato's "Dialogues." A young Italian actor was able to perform the feat of repeating a hundred lines from any of the four great Italian poets, provided he was given a line at random from their works—his hundred lines following immediately after the given line. Of course this feat required the memorizing of the entire works of those poets, and the ability to take up the repetition from any given point, the latter feature being as remarkable as the former. There have been cases of printers being able to repeat, word for word, books of which they had set the type.

A British clergyman is said to have been able to walk down a long London street, reading the names of the signs on both sides and then recalling them in the order in which they had been seen, and then by reversing the order. There are many cases on record of persons who memorized the words of every known tongue of civilization, as well as a great number of dialects, languages, and tongues of savage races. A well-known historian was once employed in a government office, the records of which were destroyed. He, thereupon, restored the entire contents of the book of records, which he had written—all from his memory.

The botanist, Asa Gray knew the names of ten thousand plants. Milton had a vocabulary of twenty thousand words, and Shakespeare one of twenty-five thousand. Magliabechi, the librarian of Florence, is said to have known the location of every volume in the large library of which he was in charge; and the complete list of works along certain lines in all the other great libraries. He once claimed that he was able to repeat titles of over a half-million of books in many languages, and upon many subjects.

In nearly every walk of life there are persons with memories wonderfully developed along the lines of their particular occupation. Librarians possess this faculty to an unusual degree. Skilled workers in the finer lines of manufacture also manifest a wonderful memory for the tiny parts of the manufactured article, etc. There are bank officers who have a wonderful memory for names and faces. Some lawyers are able to recall cases quoted in the authorities, years after they have read them. Perhaps the most common, and yet the most remarkable, instances of memorizing in one's daily work are to be found in the cases of the theatrical profession. In some cases members of stock companies must not only be able to repeat the lines of the play they are engaged in acting at the time, but also the one that they are rehearsing for the following week, and possibly the one for the second week. And in repertoire companies the actors are required to be "letter-perfect" in a dozen or more plays—surely a wonderful feat, and yet one so common that no notice is given to it.

In most retail stores today, bar codes identify and tally the prices of articles that are sold. Yet it is not uncommon for store employees of small stores whose cash registers are not computerized to know the price of every item in the store even when they change daily.

In some of the celebrated cases, the degree of recollection manifested is undoubtedly abnormal, but in the majority of the cases it may be seen that the result has been obtained only by the use of natural methods and persistent exercise. That wonderful memory may be acquired by anyone who will devote to the task patience, time and work, is a fact generally acknowledged by all students of the subject. It is not *a gift,* but something to be won by effort and work along scientific lines.

Key Points

Fabulous memories have been reported from ancient times and continue today. They are not limited to geniuses or people with in-born talent. It is manifested in people at all strata of society. Anybody with the desire to acquire this skill can do by following the principles to be discussed in the forthcoming chapters.

CHAPTER 4
MEMORY SYSTEMS

The subject of Memory Development is not a new one by any means. For two thousand years, at least, there has been much thought devoted to the subject; many books written about it, and many methods or "systems" invented, the purpose of which has been the artificial training of the memory.

Instead of endeavoring to develop the memory by scientific training and rational practice and exercise along natural lines, there seems to have always been an idea that one could improve on Nature's methods, and that a plan might be devised by the use of some "trick" the memory might be taught to give up her hidden treasures. The law of Association has been used in the majority of these systems, often to a ridiculous degree. Fanciful systems have been built up, all artificial in their character and nature, the use of which to any great extent is calculated to result in a decrease of the natural powers of remembrance and recollection, just as in the case of natural "aids" to the physical system there is always found a decrease in the natural powers. Nature prefers to do her own work, unaided. She may be trained, led, directed and harnessed, but she insists upon doing the work herself, or dropping the task.

The principle of Association is an important one, and forms a part of natural memory training, and should be so used. But when pressed into service in many of the artificial systems, the result is the erection of a complex and unnatural mental mechanism, which is no more an improvement upon the natural methods, than a wooden leg is an improvement upon the original limb. There are many points in some of these "systems" which may be employed to advantage in natural memory training, by divorcing them from their fantastic rules and complex arrangement. Let's look over the list of the principal "systems" to determine their usefulness.

The ancient Greeks were fond of memory systems. Simonides, the Greek poet who lived about 500 B.C. was one of the early authorities, and his work has influenced nearly all of the many memory systems that have sprung up since that time. There is a dramatic story connected with the foundation of his system. It is related that the poet was present at a large banquet attended by some of the principal men of the place. He was called out by a message from home, and left before the close of the meal. Shortly after he left, the ceiling of the banquet hall fell upon the guests, killing all present in the room, and mutilating their bodies so terribly that their friends were unable to recognize them. Simonides, having a well-developed memory for places and position, was able to recall the exact order in which each guest had been seated, and therefore was able to aid in the identification of the remains. This occurrence impressed him so forcibly that he devised a system of memory based upon the idea of position, which attained great popularity in Greece, and the leading writers of the day highly recommended it.

The system of Simonides was based upon the idea of position—it was known as "the topical system." His students were taught to picture in the mind a large building divided into sections, and then into rooms, halls, etc. The thing to be remembered was "visualized" as occupying some certain space or place in that building, the grouping being made according to association and resemblance. When one wished to recall the things to consciousness, all that was necessary was to visualize the mental building and then take an imaginary trip from room to room, calling off the various things as they had been placed. The Greeks thought very highly of this plan, and many variations of it were employed. Cicero said: "By those who would improve the memory, certain places must be fixed upon, and of those things which they desire to keep in memory symbols must be conceived in the mind and ranged, as it were, in those places; thus, the order of places would preserve the order of things, and the symbols of the things would denote the things themselves; so that we should use the places as waxen tablets and the symbols as letters." Another approach advises students to fix in their minds places of the greatest possible extent, diversified by considerable variety, such as a large house, for example, divided into many apartments. Whatever is remarkable in it is carefully impressed on the mind, so that the thought may run over every part of it without hesitation or delay. Places we must have, either fancied or selected, and images or symbols which we may invent at pleasure. These symbols are marks by which we may distinguish the particulars, which we have to get by heart.

Many modern systems have been erected upon the foundation of Simonides and in some of which cases students have been charged high prices "for the secret." The following example gives the "secret" of many a high priced system of this class: Select a number of rooms, and divide the walls and floor of each, in imagination, into nine equal parts or squares, three in a row, On the front wall—that opposite the entrance—of the first room, are the units; on the right-hand wall the tens; on the left hand the twenties; on the fourth wall the thirties; and on the floor the forties. Numbers 10, 20, 30 and 40, each find a place on the roof above their respective walls, while 50 occupies the center of the room. One room will thus furnish 50 places, and ten rooms as many as 500. Having fixed these clearly in the mind, so as to be able readily and at once to tell exactly the position of each place or number, it is then necessary to associate with each of them some familiar object (or symbol) so that the object being suggested its place may be instantly remembered, or when the place be before the mind its object may immediately spring up. When this has been done thoroughly, the objects can be run over in any order from beginning to end, or from end to beginning, or the place of any particular one can at once be given. All that is further necessary is to associate the ideas we wish to remember with the objects in the various places, by which means they are easily remembered, and can be gone over in any order. In this way one may learn to repeat several hundred disconnected words or ideas in any order after hearing them only once.

This system is artificial and cumbersome to a great degree. While the idea of "position" may be employed to some advantage in grouping together in the memory several associated facts, ideas, or words, still the idea of employing a process, such as the above in the ordinary affairs of life is ridiculous, and any system based upon it has a value only as a curiosity, or a mental acrobatic feat.

Akin to the above is the idea underlying many other "systems," and "secret methods"—the idea of Contiguity, in which words are strung together by fanciful connecting links. The recollection of them is assisted by associating some idea of relation between the two. We find by experience that whatever is ludicrous is calculated to make a strong impression on the mind, the more ridiculous the association is the better. The systems founded upon this idea may be employed to repeat a long string of disconnected words, and similar things, but have but little practical value, notwithstanding the high prices charged for them. They serve merely as curiosities, or methods of performing "tricks" to amuse one's friends. The above description gives the key to the principle employed. The working of the principle is accomplished by the employment of "intermediates" or "correlatives" as they are called; for instance, the words "chimney" and "leaf" would be connected as follows: "Chimney—smoke—wood—tree—Leaf."

You will find that nearly all the "systems" or "secret methods" that are being offered for sale in "courses," often at a very high price, are merely variations, improvements upon, or combinations of the forms of artificial methods named above. New changes are constantly being worked on these old plans; new tunes played on the same old instruments; new chimes sounded from the same old bells. And the result is ever the same, in these cases—disappointment and disgust. There are a few natural systems on the market, nearly all of which contain information and instruction that makes them worth the price at which they are sold. As for the others—well, judge for yourself after purchasing them, if you so desire.

Regarding these artificial and fanciful systems, all such systems for the improvement of the memory belong to what is considered the first or lowest form of it. They are for the most part based on light or foolish associations which have little foundation in nature, and are hence of little practical utility; and they do not tend to improve or strengthen the memory as a whole. These systems are barren and useless, They are an abuse of the mental powers and though they may cause admiration, they cannot be highly esteemed. The systems of mnemonics as often taught, are no better than crutches, useful to those who cannot walk, but impediments and hindrances to those who have the use of their limbs, and who only require to exercise them properly in order to have the full use of them.

Instead of trick systems the lines of natural mental action will be followed. Rather than showing you how to perform "feats" of memory; you will be instructed in the intelligent and practical use of the memory in the affairs of every day life and work.

Key Points

Instead of endeavoring to develop the memory by scientific training and rational practice and exercise along natural lines, there seems to have always been an idea that one could improve on Nature's methods, and that a plan might be devised by the use of some "trick" the memory might be taught to give up her hidden treasures.

In this book, there shall be no attempt to teach any of these "trick systems" that the student may perform for the amusement of his friends. Instead, there is only the desire to aid in developing the power to receive impressions, to register them upon the memory, and readily to reproduce them at will, naturally and easily. The lines of natural mental action will be followed throughout.

CHAPTER 5
THE SUBCONSCIOUS RECORD-FILE

The old writers on the subject considered the memory as a separate faculty of the mind, but this idea disappeared before the advancing tide of knowledge that resulted in the acceptance of the conception now known as The New Psychology. This new conception recognizes the existence of a vast "out of consciousness" region of the mind, one phase of which is known as the subconscious mind, or the subconscious field of mental activities. It is in this field, which has been called *mentation*, the activities of memory have their seat. A careful consideration of the subject brings the certainty that the entire work of the memory is performed in this subconscious region of the mind. Only when the subconscious record is represented to the conscious field, and recollection or remembrance results, does the memorized idea or impression emerge from the subconscious region. An understanding of this fact simplifies the entire subject of the memory, and enables us to perfect plans and methods whereby the memory may be developed, improved and trained, by means of the direction of the subconscious activities by the use of the conscious faculties and the will.

Memory is a faculty not only of our conscious states, but also, and much more so, of our unconscious ones. It is impossible to understand the true nature of memory, or how to train it properly, unless we have a clear conception of the fact that there is much in the mind of which we are unconscious.

The highest form of memory, as of all the mental powers, is the unconscious—when what we wish to recall comes to us spontaneously, without any conscious thought or search for it. Frequently when we wish to recall something that has previously been in the mind we are unable to do so by any conscious effort of the will; but we turn the attention to something else, and after a time the desired information comes up spontaneously when we are not consciously thinking of it. There is the working of a mechanism beneath the consciousness which, when once set going, runs on of itself, and which is more likely to evolve the desired result when the conscious activity of the mind is exerted in a direction altogether different.

This subconscious region of the mind is the great record-file of everything we have ever experienced thought or known. Everything is recorded there. The best authorities now generally agree that there is no such thing as an absolute forgetting of even the minutest impression, notwithstanding the fact that we may be unable to recollect or remember it, owing to its faintness, or lack of associated "indexing." It is held that everything is to be found in that subconscious index-file, if we can only manage to find its place. In like manner we believe that every impression or thought that has once been before consciousness remains ever afterward impressed upon the mind. It may never again come up before consciousness, but it will doubtless remain in that vast ultra-conscious region of the mind, unconsciously molding and fashioning our subsequent thoughts and actions. It is only a small part of what exists in the mind that we are conscious of. There is always much that is known to be in the mind that exists in it unconsciously, and must be stored away somewhere. We may be able to recall it into consciousness when we wish to do so; but at other times the mind is unconscious of its existence. Further, our own experience must tell us that there is much in our mind that we cannot always recall when we may wish to do so, much that we can recover only after a labored search, or that we may search for in vain at the time, but which may occur to us afterwards when perhaps we are not thinking about it. Again, much that we probably would never be able to recall, or that would not recur to us under ordinary circumstances, we may remember to have had in the mind when it is mentioned to us by others. In such a case there must still have remained some trace or scintilla of it in the mind before we could recognize it as having been there before.

We have every reason to believe that mental power when once called forth follows the analogy of everything we see in the material universe in the fact of its perpetuity. Every single effort of mind is a creation which can never go back again into nonentity. It may slumber in the depths of forgetfulness as light and heat slumber in the coal seams, but there it is, ready at the bidding of some appropriate stimulus to come again out of the darkness into the light of consciousness. That which has been long forgotten, that which we have often in vain endeavored to recollect, will sometimes without an effort of ours occur to us suddenly, and, apparently of its own accord. The mind frequently contains whole systems of knowledge which, though in our normal state they may have faded into absolute oblivion, may in certain abnormal states, as madness, delirium, somnambulism, catalepsy, etc., flash out into luminous consciousness. For example, there are cases in which the extinct memory of whole languages were suddenly restored. It is now fully established that a multitude of events which are so completely forgotten that no effort of the will can revive them, and that the statement of them calls up no reminiscences, may nevertheless be, so to speak, embedded in the memory, and may be reproduced with intense vividness under certain physical conditions.

In proof of the above, the authorities give many instances recorded in scientific annals. There is the well-known case of the old woman who could neither read nor write, who when in the delirium of fever incessantly recited in very pompous tones long passages from the Latin, Greek and Hebrew, with a distinct enunciation and precise rendition. Notes of her ravings were taken down by shorthand, and caused much wonderment, until it was afterwards found that in her youth she had been employed as a servant in the house of a clergyman who was in the habit of walking up and down in his study reading aloud from his favorite classical and religious writers. In his books were found marked passages corresponding to the notes taken from the woman's ravings. Her subconscious memory had stored up the sounds of these passages heard in her early youth, but of which she hid no recollection in her normal state. One man, describing his sensations just before being rescued from drowning says: "Every incident of my former life seemed to glance across my recollection in a retrograde procession, not in mere outline, but in a picture filled with every minute and collateral feature, thus forming a panoramic view of my whole existence."

By adopting the opinion that every thought or impression that had once been consciously before the mind is ever afterwards retained, we obtain light on many obscure mental phenomena; and especially do we draw from it the conclusion of the perfectibility of the memory to an almost unlimited extent. We cannot doubt that, could we penetrate to the lowest depths of our mental nature, we should there find traces of every impression we have received, every thought we have entertained, and every act we have done through our past life, each one making its influence felt in the way of building up our present knowledge, or in guiding our everyday actions; and if they persist in the mind, might it not be possible to recall most if not all of them into consciousness when we wished to do so, if our memories or powers of recollection were what they should be?

This great subconscious region of the mind—this Memory region—may be thought of as a great record file, with an intricate system of indexes, and data entry clerks whose business it is to file away the records; to index them; and to find them when needed. The records record only what we have impressed upon them by the attention, the degree of depth and clearness depending entirely upon the degree of attention that we bestowed upon the original impression. We can never expect to have the clerks of the memory bring up anything that they have not been given to file away. The association existing between the various impressions supplies the indexing, and cross-references. The more cross references or associations that are connected with an idea, thought or impression that is filed away in the memory, the greater the chances of it being found readily when wanted. These two features of attention and association, and the parts they play in the phenomena of memory, are mentioned in detail in other chapters of this book.

These little data entry clerks of the memory are an industrious and willing lot of workers, but like all workers they do their best work when kept in practice. Idleness and lack of exercise cause them to become slothful and careless, and forgetful of the records under their charge. A little fresh exercise and work soon take the cobwebs out of their brains, and they spring eagerly to their tasks. They become familiar with their work when exercised properly, and soon become very expert. They have a tendency to remember, on their own part, and when a certain record is called for often they grow accustomed to its place, and can find it without referring to the indexes at all. But their trouble comes from faint and almost illegible records, caused by poor attention—these they can scarcely decipher when they do succeed in finding them. Lack of proper indexing by associations causes them much worry and extra work, and some-times they are unable to find the records at all from this neglect. Often, however, after they have told you that they could not find a thing, and you have left the place in disgust, they will continue their search and hours afterward will surprise you by handing you the desired idea, or impression, which they had found carelessly indexed or improperly filed away. In these chapters you will be helped, if you will carry in your mind these custodians of the memory record file, and the hard work they have to do for you, much of which is made doubly burdensome by your own neglect and carelessness. Treat these clerks right and they will work overtime for you, willingly and joyfully. But they need your assistance and encouragement, and an occasional word of praise and com-mendation.

Key Points

The entire work of the memory is performed in this subconscious region of the mind. Only when the subconscious record is represented to the conscious field, and recollection or remembrance results, does the memorized idea or impression emerge from the subconscious region. An understanding of this fact simplifies the entire subject of the memory, and enables us to perfect plans and methods whereby the memory may be developed, improved and trained, by means of the direction of the subconscious activities by the use of the conscious faculties and the will.

By adopting the opinion that every thought or impression that had once been consciously before the mind is ever afterwards retained, we obtain light on many obscure mental phenomena; and especially do we draw from it the conclusion of the perfectibility of the memory to an almost unlimited extent.

CHAPTER 6

ATTENTION

As we have seen in the preceding chapters, before we can expect to recall or remember a thing, that thing must have been impressed upon the records of our subconscious mind, distinctly and clearly. The main factor of the recording of impressions is that quality of the mind that is called *Attention*. All the leading authorities on the subject of memory recognize and teach the value of attention in the cultivation and development of the memory. The great art of memory is attention. Inattentive people have always have poor memories. It is generally held by philosophers that without some degree of attention no impression of any duration could be made on the mind, or laid up in the memory.

It is a law of the mind that the intensity of the present consciousness determines the vivacity of the future memory; memory and consciousness are thus in the direct ratio of each other: vivid consciousness, long memory; faint consciousness, short memory; no consciousness, no memory. An act of attention, that is an act of concentration, is necessary to every exertion of consciousness, as a certain contraction of the pupil is requisite to every exertion of vision. Attention, then, is to consciousness what the contraction of the pupil is to sight, or to the eye of the mind what the microscope or telescope is to the bodily eye. It constitutes the better half of all intellectual power.

The subconscious regions of the mind are the great store-houses of the mental records of impressions from within and without. Its great systems of filing, recording and index-ing these records constitute memory. But before any of this work is possible, impressions must first have been received. These impressions depend upon the power of attention given to the things making the impressions. If great attention has been given, there will be clear and deep impressions; if only average attention has been given, there will be but average impressions; if only faint attention has been given, there will be but faint impressions; if no attention has been given, there will be no records.

One of the most common causes of poor attention is to be found in the lack of interest. We are apt to remember the things in which we have been most interested, because in that outpouring of interest there has been a high degree of attention manifested. There are people who may have a very poor memory for many things, but when it comes to the things in which their interest is involved they often remember the minutest details. What is called involuntary attention is that form of attention that follows upon inter-est, curiosity, or desire—no special effort of the will being required in it. What is called voluntary attention is that form of attention that is bestowed upon objects not necessarily interesting, curious, or attractive—this requires the application of the will, and is a mark of a developed character. Every person has more or less involuntary attention, while but few possess developed voluntary attention. The former is instinctive—the latter comes only by practice and training.

But there is this important point to be remembered, that *interest may be developed by voluntary attention* bestowed and held upon an object. Things that are originally lacking in sufficient interest to attract the involuntary attention may develop a secondary interest if the voluntary attention were placed upon and held upon them. When it is said that attention will not take a firm hold on an uninteresting thing, we must not forget that anyone not shallow and fickle can soon discover something interesting in most objects. Here cultivated minds show their especial superiority, for the attention that they are able to give generally ends in finding a pearl in the most uninteresting looking oyster. When an object necessarily loses interest from one point of view, such minds discover in it new attributes. The essence of genius is to present an old thing in new ways, whether it is some force in nature or some aspect of humanity.

It is very difficult to teach another person how to cultivate the attention. This is because the whole thing consists so largely in the use of the will, and by faithful practice and persistent application. The first requisite is *the determination to use the will*. You must argue it out with yourself, until you become convinced that it is necessary and desirable for you to acquire the art of voluntary attention—you must convince yourself beyond reasonable doubt. This is the first step and one more difficult than it would seem at first sight. The principal difficulty in it lies in the fact that to do the thing you must do some active earnest thinking, and the majority of people are too lazy to indulge in such mental effort. Having mastered this first step, you must induce a strong burning desire to acquire the art of voluntary attention—you must learn to want it hard. In this way you induce a condition of interest and attractiveness where it was previously lacking. Third and last, you must hold your will firmly and persistently to the task, and practice faithfully.

Begin by turning your attention upon some uninteresting thing and studying its details until you are able to describe them. This will prove very tiresome at first but you must stick to it. Do not practice too long at a time at first; take a rest and try it again later. You will soon find that it comes easier, and that a new interest is beginning to manifest itself in the task. Examine this book, as practice, learn how many pages there are in it; how many chapters; how many pages in each chapter; the details of type, printing and binding—all the little things about it—so that you could give another person a full account of the minor details of the book. This may seem uninteresting—and so it will be at first—but a little practice will create a new interest in the petty details, and you will be surprised at the number of little things that you will notice. This plan, practiced on many things, in spare hours, will develop the power of voluntary attention and perception in anyone, no matter how deficient he may have been in these things. If you can get some one else to join in the game-task with you and then each endeavor to excel the other in finding details, the task will be much easier, and better work will be accomplished. Begin to take notice of things about you; the places you visit; the things in the rooms, etc. In this way you will start the habit of "noticing things," which is the first requisite for memory development.

To look at a thing intelligently is the most difficult of all arts. The first rule for the cultivation of accurate perception is: Do not try to perceive the whole of a complex object at once. Take the human face as an example. A man, holding an important position to which he had been elected, offended many people because he could not remember faces, and hence failed to recognize individuals the second time he met them. His trouble was in looking at the countenance as a whole. When he changed his method of observation, and noticed carefully the nose, mouth, eyes, chin, and color of hair, he at once began to find recognition easier. He was no longer in difficulty of mistaking A for B, since he remembered that the shape of B's nose was different, or the color of his hair at least three shades lighter.

This example shows that another rule can be formulated: Pay careful attention to details. We are perhaps asked to give a minute description of the exterior of a somewhat noted suburban house that we have lately seen. We reply in general terms, giving the size and color of the house. Perhaps we also have an idea of part of the material used in the exterior construction. We are asked to be exact about the shape of the door, porch, roof, chimneys and windows; whether the windows are plain or circular, whether they have cornices, or whether the trimmings around them are of the same material as the rest of the house. A friend, who will be unable to see the house, wishes to know definitely about the angles of the roof, and the way the windows are arranged with reference to them. Unless we can answer these questions exactly, we merely tantalize our friends by telling them we have seen the house. To see an object merely as an indiscriminate mass of something in a certain place, is to do no more than a donkey accomplishes as he trots along.

There are three general rules that may be given in this matter of bestowing the voluntary attention in the direction of actually *seeing* things, instead of merely looking at them. The first is: Make yourself take an interest in the thing. The second: See it as if you were taking note of it in order to repeat its details to a friend—this will force you to "take notice." The third: Give to your subconsciousness a mental command to take note of what you are looking at—say to it; "Here, you take note of this and remember it for me!" This last consists of a peculiar "knack" that can be attained by a little practice—it will "come to you" suddenly after a few trials.

The third rule, making the subconsciousness work for you, can be illustrated by a curious fact in physics. If you wished to ring a bell so as to produce as much sound as possible, you would probably pull it as far back as you could, and then let it go. But if you would, in letting it go, simply give it a tap with your forefinger, you would actually redouble the sound. Or, to shoot an arrow as far as possible, it is not enough to *merely* draw the bow to its utmost span or tension. If, just as it goes, you will give the bow a quick push, though the effort be trifling, the arrow will fly almost as far again as it would have done without it. Or, if, as is well known in wielding a very sharp saber, we make the draw cut; that is, if to the blow or chop, as with an axe, we also add a certain slight pull, simultaneously, we can cut through a silk handkerchief or a sheep. Forethought (command to the subconsciousness) is the tap on the bell; the push on the bow; the draw on the saber. It is the deliberate but yet rapid action of the mind when before dismissing thought; we bid the mind to consequently respond. It is more than merely thinking what we are to do; it is the bidding or ordering the self to fulfill a task before willing it.

Remember first, last and always, that before you can remember, or recollect, you must first *perceive;* and that perception is possible only through attention, and responds in degree to the latter. Therefore, it has truly been said that: "The great Art of Memory is Attention."

Key Points

The subconscious regions of the mind are the great storehouses of the mental records of impressions from within and without.

One of the most common causes of poor attention is to be found in the lack of interest. We are apt to remember the things in which we have been most interested, because in that outpouring of interest there has been a high degree of attention given.

Interest may be developed by voluntary attention bestowed and held upon an object.

The three requisites of cultivating attention:

Determine to use the will.

Develop strong burning desire to acquire the art of voluntary attention.

Practice this faithfully.

There are three general rules that may be given in this matter of bestowing the voluntary attention in the direction of actually *seeing* things, instead of merely looking at them. The first is: Make yourself take an interest in the thing. The second: See it as if you were taking note of it in order to repeat its details to a friend—this will force you to "take notice." The third: Give to your subconsciousness a mental command to take note of what you are looking at.

Remember first, last and always, that before you can remember, or recollect, you must first *perceive;* and that perception is possible only through attention and responds in degree to the latter.

CHAPTER 7
ASSOCIATION

In the preceding chapters we have seen that in order that a thing may be remembered, it must be impressed clearly upon the mind in the first place; and that in order to obtain a clear impression there must be a manifestation of attention. So much for the recording of the impressions, but when we come to recalling, recollecting or remembering the impressions we are brought face to face with another important law of memory—the law of Association.

Association plays a part analogous to the indexing and cross-indexing of a book; a library; or another system in which the aim is to readily find something that has been filed away, or contained in some way in a collection of similar things. In order that what is in the memory may be recalled or brought again before consciousness, it is necessary that it be regarded in connection, or in association with one or more other things or ideas, and as a rule the greater the number of other things with which it is associated the greater the likelihood of its recall. The two processes are involved in every act of memory. We must first impress, and then we must associate. Without a clear impression being formed, that which is recalled will be indistinct and inaccurate; and unless it is associated with something else in the mind, it cannot be recalled. If we may suppose an idea existing in the mind by itself, unconnected with any other idea, its recall would be impossible.

The recording power of memory mainly depends upon the degree of attention we give to the idea to be remembered. The reproducing power again altogether depends upon the nature of the associations by *which* the new idea has been linked on to other ideas that have been previously recorded.

The most fundamental law that regulates psychological phenomena is the law of association. In its comprehensive character it is comparable to the law of attraction in the physical world. That which the law of gravitation is to astronomy; that which the elementary properties of the tissues are to physiology; the law of association of ideas is to psychology.

The connection between memory and the association of ideas is so striking that it has been supposed by some that the whole of the phenomena might be resolved into this principle. The association of ideas connects our various thoughts with each other, so as to present them to the mind in a certain order. But it presupposes the existence of those thoughts in the mind—in other words it presupposes a faculty of retaining the knowledge that we acquire. On the other hand, it is evident that without the associating

principle, the power of retaining our thoughts, and of recognizing them when they occur to us, would have been of
little use; for the most important articles of our knowledge
might have remained latent in the mind, even when those
occasions presented themselves to which they were immediately applicable.

Association of ideas depends upon two principles known,
respectively, as (1) the law of contiguity; and (2) the law of
similarity. Association by contiguity is that form of association by which an idea is linked, connected, or associated
with the sensation, thought, or idea immediately preceding
it, and that, which directly follows it. Each idea, or thought,
is a link in a great chain of thought being connected with
the preceding link and the succeeding link. Association
by similarity is that form of association by which an idea,
thought, or sensation is linked, connected, or associated
with ideas, thoughts, or sensations of a similar kind, which
have occurred previously or subsequently. The first form of
association is the relation of sequence—the second the relation of kind.

Association by contiguity is the great law of thought, as
well as of memory. The connection that naturally subsists
between a sensation and idea in the mind, and that, which
immediately preceded or followed it, is of the strongest and
most intimate nature. The two, strictly speaking, are but one,
forming one complete thought. To speak correctly, there is
no isolated or separate sensation. A sensation is a state which
begins as a continuation of preceding ones, and ends by losing itself in those following it; it is by an arbitrary severing,
and for the convenience of language, that we set it apart as

we do; its beginning is the end of another, and its ending the beginning of another. When we read or hear a sentence, for example, at the commencement of the fifth word something of the fourth word still remains. Association by contiguity may be separated into two sub-classes—contiguity in time; and contiguity in space. In contiguity in time there is manifested the tendency of the memory to recall the impressions in the same order in which they were received—the first impression suggesting the second, and that the third, and so on. In this way the child learns to repeat the alphabet and the adult the succeeding lines of a poem. In a poem, the end of each preceding word being connected with the beginning of the succeeding one, we can easily repeat them in that order, but we are not able to repeat them backwards till they have been frequently named in that order. Memory of words, or groups of words, depends upon this form of contiguous association. Some persons are able to repeat long poems from beginning to end, with perfect ease, but are unable to repeat any particular sentence, or verse, without working down to it from the beginning. Contiguity in space is manifested in forms of recollection or remembrance by "position." Thus by remembering the things connected with the position of a particular thing, we are enabled to recall the thing itself. As we have seen in a preceding chapter, some forms of memory systems have been based on this law. If you will recall some house or room in which you have been, you will find that you will remember one object after another, in the order of the relative positions, or contiguity in space, or position. Beginning with the front hall, you may travel in memory from one room to another, recalling each with the objects it contains, according to the degree of attention you bestowed upon them originally. It is on this principle of contiguity that mnemonical systems are constructed, as when what we wish to remember is associated in the mind with a certain object or locality, the ideas associated will at once come up; or when each word or idea is associated with the one immediately preceding it, so that when the one is recalled the other comes up along with it, and thus long lists of names or long passages of books can be readily learned by heart.

From the foregoing, it will be seen that it is of great importance that we correlate our impressions with those preceding and following. The more closely knitted together our impressions are, the more closely will they cohere, and the greater will be the facility of remembering or recollecting them. We should endeavor to form our impressions of things so that they will be associated with other impressions, in time and space. Every other thing that is associated in the mind with a given thing, serves as a "loose end" of memory, which if once grasped and followed up will lead us to the thing we desire to recall to mind.

Association by similarity is the linking together of impressions of a similar kind, irrespective of time and place. The law of similarity expresses the general fact that any present state of consciousness tends to revive previous states that are similar to it. Rational or philosophical association is when a fact or statement on which the attention is fixed is associated with some fact previously known, to which it has a relation, or with some subject which it is calculated to illustrate. The similars may be widely apart in space or in time, but they are brought together and associated through their resemblance to each other. Thus, a circumstance of today may recall circumstances of a similar nature that occurred perhaps at very different times, and they will become associated together in the mind, so that afterwards the presence of one will tend to recall the others. The habit of correct association—that is, connecting facts in the mind according to their true relations, and to the manner in which they tend to illustrate each other, is one of the principle means of improving the memory, particularly that kind of memory which is an essential quality of a cultivated mind—namely, that which is founded not upon incidental connections, but on true and important relations.

The more relations or likenesses that we find or can establish between objects, the more easily will the view of one lead us to recollect the rest. In order to fix a thing in the memory, we must associate it with something in the mind already, and the more closely that which we wish to remember resembles that with which it is associated, the better it is fixed in the memory, and the more readily is it recalled. If the two strongly resemble each other, or are not to be distinguished from each other, then the association is of the strongest kind. The memory is able to retain and replace a vastly greater number of ideas, if they are associated or arranged on some principle of similarity, than if they are presented merely as isolated facts. It is not by the multitude of ideas, but the want of arrangement among them, that the memory burdened and its powers weakened.

Acquaint yourself with the general idea of the working features of the law of association as given in this chapter for the reason that much of the instruction to be given under the head of the several phases and classes of memory is based upon an application of the Law of Association, in connection with the law of Attention. These fundamental principles should be clearly grasped before you can proceed to the details of practice and exercise. You should know not only *how* to use the mind and memory in certain ways, but also *why* it is to be used in that particular way. By understanding the *reason of it,* you will be better able to follow out the directions.

Key Points

Association by contiguity is that form of association by which an idea is linked, connected, or associated with the sensation, thought, or idea immediately preceding it, and that, which directly follows it. Each idea, or thought, is a link in a great chain of thought being connected with the preceding link and the succeeding link. Association by similarity is that form of association by which an idea, thought, or sensation is linked, connected, or associated with ideas, thoughts, or sensations of a similar kind, which have occurred previously or subsequently. The first form of association is the relation of sequence—the second the relation of kind.

In order that what is in the memory may be recalled or brought again before consciousness, it is necessary that it be regarded in connection, or in association with one or more other things or ideas, and as a rule the greater the number of other things with which it is associated the greater the likelihood of its recall. The two processes are involved in every act of memory. We must first impress, and then we must associate. Without a clear impression being formed, that which is recalled will be indistinct and inaccurate; and unless it is associated with something else in the mind, it cannot be recalled. If we may suppose an idea existing in the mind by itself, unconnected with any other idea, its recall would be impossible.

Association by similarity is the linking together of impressions of a similar kind, irrespective of time and place. The law of similarity expresses the general fact that any present state of consciousness tends to revive previous states that are similar to it.

You should know not only *how* to use the mind and memory in certain ways, but also *why* it is to be used in that particular way. By understanding the *reason of it,* you will be better able to follow out the directions.

CHAPTER 8

PHASES OF MEMORY

One of the first things apt to be noticed when you study memory is the fact that there are several different phases of the manifestation of memory. That is to say, that there are several general classes into which the phenomena of memory may be grouped. And accordingly we find some persons quite highly developed in certain phases of memory, and quite deficient in others. If there were but one phase or class of memory, then a person who had developed his memory along any particular line would have at the same time developed it equally along all the other lines. But this is far from being the true state of affairs. We find people who are quite proficient in recalling the impression of faces, while they find it very *difficult* to recall the names of the persons whose faces they remember. Others can remember faces, and not names. Others have an excellent recollection of localities, while others are constantly losing themselves.

Others remember dates, prices, numbers, and figures generally, while deficient in other forms of recollection. Others remember tales, incidents, anecdotes etc., while forgetting other things and so on, Each one of us is apt to possess a memory good in some phases, while deficient in others.

The phases of memory may be divided into two general classes, namely (1) Memory of Sense Impressions; and (2) Memory of Ideas. This classification is somewhat arbitrary, for the reason that sense impressions develop into ideas, and ideas are composed to a considerable extent of sense impressions, but in a general way the classification serves its purpose, which is the grouping together of certain phases of the phenomena of memory.

Memory of Sense Impressions of course includes the impressions received from all of the five senses, sight, hearing, taste, touch and smell. But when we come down to a practical examination of sense impressions retained in the memory, we find that the majority of such impressions are those obtained through the two respective senses of sight and hearing.

The impressions received from the sense of taste, touch and smell, respectively, are comparatively small, except in the cases of certain experts in special lines, whose occupation consists in acquiring a very delicate sense of taste, smell or touch, and correspondingly a fine sense of memory along these particular lines. For instance, the wine-taster and tea-tasters, who are able to distinguish between the various grades of merchandise handled by them, have developed not only very fine senses of taste and smell, but also a remarkable memory of the impressions previously received, the power of discrimination depending as much upon the memory as upon the special sense. In the same way the skilled surgeon as well as the skilled mechanic acquires a fine sense of touch and a correspondingly highly developed memory of touch impressions.

The greater part of the sense impressions stored away in our memories are those previously received through the senses of sight and hearing, respectively. The majority of sense impressions, stored away in the memory, have been received more or less involuntarily, that is with the application of but a slight degree of attention. They are more or less indistinct and hazy, and are recalled with difficulty, the remembrance of them generally coming about without conscious effort, according to the law of association. That is, they come principally when we are thinking about something else upon which we have given thought and attention, and with which they have been associated. There is quite a difference between the remembrance of sense impressions received in this way, and those that we record by the bestowal of attention, interest and concentration.

The sense impressions of sight are by far the most numerous in our subconscious storehouse. We are constantly exercising our sense of sight, and receiving thousands of different sight impressions every hour. However, the majority of these impressions are but faintly recorded upon the memory. We give to them but little attention or interest. But it is astonishing, at times, when we find that when we recall some important event or incident we also recall many faint sight impressions of which we did not dream we had any record.

To realize the important part played by sight impressions in the phenomena of memory, recall some particular time or event in your life, and see how many more things that you remembered, compared with the number of things that you *heard,* or tasted, or felt or smelled.

Second in number, however, are the impressions received through the sense of hearing, and consequently the memory stores away a great number of sound impressions. In some cases the impressions of sight and sound are joined together, as for instance in the case of words, in which not only the sound but the shape of the letters composing the word, or rather the word-shape itself, are stored away together, and consequently are far more readily remembered or recollected than things of which but one sense impression is recorded. Teachers of memory use this fact as a means of helping their students to memorize words by speaking them aloud, and then writing them down. Many persons memorize names in this way, the impression of the written word being added to the impression of the sound, thus doubling the record. The more impressions that you can make regarding a thing, the greater are the chances of your easily recollecting it. Likewise it is very important to attach an impression of a weaker sense, to that of a stronger one, in order that the former may be memorized. For instance, if you have a good eye memory, and a poor ear memory, it is well to attach your sound impressions to the sight impressions. And if you have a poor eye memory, and a good ear memory it is important to attach your sight impressions to your sound impressions. In this way you take advantage of the law of association.

Under the sub-class of sight impressions, are found the smaller divisions of memory known as memory of locality; memory of figures; memory of form; memory of color; and memory of written or printed words. Under the sub-class of sound impressions are found the smaller divisions of memory known as memory of spoken words: memory of names; memory of stories; memory of music, etc. Special attention will be given to these forms of memory in succeeding chapters.

The second general class of memory—memory of ideas—includes the memory of facts, events, thoughts, lines of reasoning, etc., and is regarded as higher in the scale than the memory of sense impressions, although not more necessary nor useful to the average person. This form of memory of course accompanies the higher lines of intellectual effort and activities, and constitutes a large part of what is known as true education, that is education which teaches one to think instead of to merely memorize certain things taught in books or lectures.

Well-rounded people mentally, are those who have developed their memory on all sides, rather than those who have developed but one special phase of the faculty. It is true that your interest and occupation certainly tend to develop your memory according to your daily needs and requirements, but it is well that you should give to the other parts of your memory field some exercise, in order that you may not grow one-sided. Many persons think that memory is mainly due to sight; but we have as many different kinds of memory as we have senses. To sight, the watermelon is a long greenish body, but this is its least important quality. Sight alone gives the poorest idea of the watermelon. We approach the vine where the fruit is growing, and in order to decide whether it is ripe, we tap the rind and judge by the sound. We must remember that a ripe watermelon has a certain resonance. By passing our hands over the melon, we learn that it has certain touch characteristics. We cut it open and learn the qualities of taste and smell. All this knowledge afforded by the different senses must enter into a perfected memory image. Many complex processes go to form an idea of a thing. Napoleon was not content with only hearing a name. He wrote it down, and having satisfied his eye memory as well as his ear memory, he threw the paper away.

In this book you will learn the methods and processes calculated to round out your memory. As a rule your strong phases of memory need but little attention; although even in these a little scientific knowledge will be of use. But in the weaker phases, those phases in which your memory is "poor," you should exert a new energy and activity, to the end that these weaker regions of the memory may be cultivated and fertilized, and well stored with the seed impressions, which will bear a good crop in time. There is no phase, field, or class of memory that is not capable of being highly developed by intelligent application. It requires practice, exercise and work—but the reward is great. Many people are handicapped by being deficient in certain phases of memory, while proficient in others. The remedy is in your own hands, and in this book you will be given the means to acquire a "good" memory along any or all lines.

Key Points

The phases of memory may be divided into two general classes, namely (1) Memory of Sense Impressions; and (2) Memory of Ideas.

Memory of Sense Impressions of course includes the impressions received from all of the five senses: sight, hearing, taste, touch and smell. But when we come down to a practical examination of sense impressions retained in the memory, we find that the majority of such impressions are those obtained through the two respective senses of sight and hearing.

The more impressions that you can make regarding a thing, the greater are the chances of your easily recollecting it. Likewise it is very important to attach an impression of a weaker sense, to that of a stronger one, in order that the former may be memorized. For instance, if you have a good eye memory, and a poor ear memory, it is well to attach your sound impressions to the sight impressions. And if you have a poor eye memory, and a good ear memory it is important to attach your sight impressions to your sound impressions. There is no phase, field, or class of memory that is not capable of being highly developed It requires practice, exercise and work.

CHAPTER 9

TRAINING THE EYE

Before the memory can be stored with sight impressions—before the mind can recollect or remember such impressions—the eye must be used under the direction of the attention. We think that we see things when we look at them, but in reality we *see* but few things, in the sense of registering clear and distinct impressions of them upon the tablets of the subconscious mind. We *look at* them rather than *see* them.

A body may be imaged on the retina without insuring perception. There must be an effort to concentrate the attention upon the many things that the world presents to our senses. A teacher once said to the pupils of a large school, all of whom had seen cows: I should like to find out how many of you know whether a cow's ears are above, below, behind, or in front of her horns. I want only those pupils to raise their hands who are sure about the position and who will promise to give a dollar to charity if they answer wrong.

Only two hands were raised. Their owners had drawn cows and in order to do that had been forced to concentrate their attention upon the animals. Fifteen pupils were sure that they had seen cats climb trees and descend them. There was unanimity of opinion that the cats went up heads first. When asked whether the cats came down head or tail first, the majority was sure that the cats descended, as they were never known to do. Any one who had ever noticed the shape of the claws of any beast of prey could have answered the question without seeing an actual descent. Farmers' boys who have often seen cows and horses lie down and rise, are seldom sure whether the animals rise with their fore or hind feet first, or whether the habit of the horse agrees with that of the cow in this respect. The elm tree has about its leaf a peculiarity which all *ought to* notice the first time they see it, and yet only about five per cent of a certain school could incorporate in a drawing this peculiarity, although it is so easily outlined on paper. Perception, to achieve satisfactory results, must summon the will to its aid to concentrate the attention. Only the smallest part of what falls upon our senses at any time is actually perceived.

The way to train the mind to receive clear sight-impressions, and therefore to retain them in the memory is simply to concentrate the will and attention upon objects of sight, endeavoring to *see* them plainly and distinctly, and then to practice recalling the details of the object some time afterward. It is astonishing how rapidly one may improve in this respect by a little practice. And it is amazing how great a degree of proficiency in this practice one may attain in a short time.

Houdin, the French conjurer cultivated his memory of sight impressions by following a simple plan. He started to practice by observing the number of small objects in the Paris shop windows he could see and remember in one quick glance as he rapidly walked past the window. He followed the plan of noting down on paper the things that he saw and remembered. At first he could remember but two or three articles in the window. Then he began to see and remember more, and so on, each day adding to his power of perception and memory, until finally he was able to see and remember nearly every small article in a large shop window, after only one glance upon it. Others have found this plan an excellent one, and have developed their power of perception greatly, and at the same time cultivated an amazingly retentive memory of objects seen. It is all a matter of use and practice. The experiment of Houdin may be varied infinitely, with excellent results.

The Hindus train their children by playing the "sight game" with them. This game is played by exposing to the sight of the children a number of small objects, at which they gaze intently, and which are then withdrawn from their sight. The children then endeavor to excel each other in writing down the names of the objects that they have seen. The number of objects is small to begin with, but is increased each day, until an astonishing number are perceived and remembered.

Rudyard Kipling in his great book, "Kim," gives an instance of this game, played by Kim and a trained native youth. Lurgan Sahib exposes to the sight of the two boys a tray filled with jewels and gems, allowing them to gaze upon it a few moments before it is withdrawn from sight. Then the competition begins, as follows: "There are under that paper five blue stones, one big, one smaller, and three small," said Kim in all haste. "There are four green stones, and one with a hole in it; there is one yellow stone that I can see through, and one like a pipe stem. There are two red stones, and—and give me time." But Kim had reached the limit of his powers. Then the native boy had his turn. "Hear my count," cried the native child. "First are two flawed sapphires, one of two ruttes (an old Asian means of weighing gems) and one of four, as I should judge. The four rutte sapphire is chipped at the edge. There is one Turkestan turquoise, plain with green veins, and there are two inscribed—one with the name of God in gilt, and the other being cracked across, for it came out of an old ring, I cannot read. We have now the five blue stones; four flamed emeralds there are, but one is drilled in two places, and one is a little carven weight?" asked Lurgan Sahib, impassively. "Three—five—five and four ruttees, as I judge it. There is one piece of old greenish amber, and a cheap cut topaz from Europe. There is one ruby of Burma, one of two ruttees, without a flaw. And there is a ballas ruby, flawed, of two ruttees. There is a carved ivory from China, representing a rat sucking an egg; and there is last—Ah—ha!—a ball of crystal as big as a bean set in gold leaf." Kim is mortified at his bad beating, and asks the secret. The answer is: "By doing it many times over, till it is done perfectly, for it is worth doing."

Many teachers have followed plans similar to that just related. A number of small articles are exposed, and the pupils are trained to see and remember them, the process being gradually made more and more difficult. A well-known American teacher was in the habit of rapidly making a number of dots on the blackboard, and then erasing them before the pupils could count them in the ordinary way. The children then endeavored to count their mental impressions, and before long they could correctly name the number up to ten or more, with ease. They said they could "see six," or "see ten," as the case may be, automatically and apparently without the labor of consciously counting them.

It is related in works dealing with the detection of crime, that in the celebrated "thieves schools" in Europe, the young thieves are trained in a similar way, the old scoundrels acting as teachers exposing a number of small articles to the young ones, and requiring them to repeat exactly what they had seen. Then follows a higher course in which the young thieves are required to memorize the objects in a room; the plan of houses, etc. They are sent forth to "spy out the land" for future robberies, in the guise of beggars soliciting alms, and thus getting a rapid peep into houses, offices, and stores. It is said that in a single glance they will perceive the location of all of the doors, windows, locks, bolts, etc.

Many nations have boys' games in which the youngsters are required to see and remember after taking a peep. The Italians have a game called "Morro" in which one player throws out a number of fingers, which must be instantly named by the other player, a failure resulting in a forfeit. The Chinese youths have a similar game, while the Japanese reduce this to a science. A well-trained Japanese youth will be able to remember the entire contents of a room after one keen glance around it. Many of the Asians have developed this faculty to a degree almost beyond belief. But the principle is the same in all cases—the gradual practice and exercise, beginning with a small number of simple things, and then increasing the number and complexity of the objects.

The faculty is not as rare as one might imagine at first thought. Take an owner in a small business, and let him or her enter the store of a competitor, and see how many things that will be observed and remembered after a few minutes in the place. Let an actor visit a play in another theatre, and see how many details of the performance he will notice and remember. Let some women pay a visit to a new neighbor, and then see how many things about that house they will have seen and remembered, to be retailed to their confidential friends afterward.

It is the old story of attention following the interest, and memory following the attention. An expert bridge player will see and remember every card played in the game, and just who played it. A chess or checker player will see and remember the previous moves in the game, and an expert, can relate them afterward. A woman will go shopping and will see and remember thousands of things that a man would never have seen, much less remembered. The French conjuror, Houdin commented: "I can safely assert that a lady seeing another pass at full speed in a carriage will have had time to analyze her toilette from her bonnet to her shoes, and be able to describe not only the fashion and quality of the stuffs, but also say if the lace be real or only machine made. I have known ladies to do this."

But, remember this—for it is important: Whatever can be done in this direction by means of attention, inspired by interest, may be duplicated by *attention directed by will*. In other words, the desire to accomplish the task adds and creates an artificial interest just as effective as the natural feeling. And, as you progress, the interest in the game-task will add new interest, and you will be able to duplicate any of the feats mentioned above. It is all a matter of attention, interest (natural or induced) and practice. Begin with a set of dominoes, if you like, and try to remember the spots on one of them rapidly glanced at, then two, then three. By increasing the number gradually, you will attain a power of perception and a memory of sight-impressions that will appear almost marvelous. And not only will you begin to remember dominoes, but you will also be able to perceive and remember thousands of little details of interest, in everything, that have heretofore escaped your notice. The principle is very simple, but the results that may be obtained by practice are wonderful.

The trouble with most of you is that you have been looking without seeing—gazing but not observing. The objects around you have been out of your mental focus. If you will but change your mental focus, by means of will and attention, you will be able to cure yourself of the careless methods of seeing and observing that have been hindrances to your success. You have been blaming it on your memory, but the fault is with your perception. How can the memory remember, when it is not given anything in the way of clear impressions. You have been like young infants in this matter—now it is time for you to begin to sit up and take notice, no matter how old you may be. The whole thing in a nutshell is this: In order to remember the things that pass before your sight, you must begin to *see with your mind,* instead of with your retina. Let the impression get beyond your retina and into your mind.

Key Points

Perception, to achieve satisfactory results, must summon the will to its aid to concentrate the attention. Only the smallest part of what falls upon our senses at any time is actually perceived."

The way to train the mind to receive clear sight-impressions, and therefore to retain them in the memory is simply to concentrate the will and attention upon objects of sight, endeavoring to *see* them plainly and distinctly, and then to practice recalling the details of the object some time afterward.

The desire to accomplish the task adds and creates an artificial interest just as effective as the natural feeling. It is all a matter of attention, interest (natural or induced) and practice.

By changing your mental focus, by means of will and attention, you will be able to cure yourself of the careless methods of seeing and observing that have been hindrances to your success. You have been blaming it on your memory, but the fault is with your perception.

In order to remember the things that pass before your sight, you must begin to *see with your mind,* instead of with your retina. Let the impression get beyond your retina and into your mind.

CHAPTER 10

TRAINING THE EAR

The sense of hearing is one of the highest of the senses or channels whereby we receive impressions from the outside world. In fact, it ranks almost as high as the sense of sight. In the senses of taste, touch, and smell there is a direct contact between the sensitive recipient nerve substance and the particles of the object sensed, while in the sense of sight and the sense of hearing the impression is received through the medium of waves in the atmosphere (in the case of sight), or waves in the air (in the sense of hearing.) Moreover in taste, smell and touch the objects sensed are brought into direct contact with the terminal nerve apparatus, while in seeing and hearing the nerves terminate in peculiar and delicate sacs which contain a fluidic substance through which the impression is conveyed to the nerve proper. Loss of this fluidic substance destroys the faculty to receive impressions, and deafness or blindness ensues.

Just as it is true that it is the mind and not the eye that really *sees; so is* it true that it is the mind and not the ear that really *hears.* Many sounds reach the ears that are not registered by the mind. We pass along a crowded street, the waves of many sounds reaching the nerves of the ear, and yet the mind *accepts* the sounds of but few things, particularly when the novelty of the sounds has passed away. It is a matter of interest and attention in this case, as well as in the case of hearing. For example, If we sit by an open window in the country on a summer day, we may have many stimuli knocking at the gate of attention: the ticking of a clock, the sound of the wind, the cackling of fowl, the quacking of ducks, the barking of dogs, the lowing of cows, the cries of children at play, the rustling of leaves, the songs of birds, the rumbling of wagons, etc. If attention is centered upon any one of these that for the time being acquires the importance of a king upon the throne of our mental world.

Many persons complain of not being able to remember sounds, or things reaching the mind through the sense of hearing, and attribute the trouble to some defect in the organs of hearing. But in so doing they overlook the real cause of the trouble, for it is a scientific fact that many of such persons are found to have hearing apparatus perfectly developed and in the best working order. Their trouble arises from a lack of training of the mental faculty of hearing. In other words the trouble is in their mind instead of in the organs of hearing. To acquire the faculty of correct hearing, and correct memory of things heard, the mental faculty of hearing must be exercised, trained and developed. Given a number of people whose hearing apparatus are equally perfect, we will find that some "hear" much better than others; and some hear certain things better than they do certain other things; and that there is a great difference in the grades and degrees of memory of the things heard. Great differences exist among individuals with regard to the acuteness of the sense of hearing and some possess it in greater perfection in certain directions than in others. One whose hearing is good for sound in general may yet have but little ear for musical tones. On the other hand, one with a good ear for music may yet be deficient as regards hearing in general. The secret of this is to be found in the degree of interest and attention bestowed upon the particular thing giving forth the sound.

It is a fact that the mind will hear the faintest sounds from things in which is centered interest and attention, while at the same time ignoring things in which there is no interest and to which the attention is not turned. A sleeping mother will awaken at the slightest whimper from her baby, while the rumbling of a heavy wagon on the street, or even the discharge of a gun in the neighborhood may not be noticed by her. An engineer will detect the slightest difference in the whir or hum of an engine, while failing to notice a very loud noise outside. A musician will note the slightest discord occurring in a concert in which there are a great number of instruments being played, and in which there is a great volume of sound reaching the ear, while other sounds may be unheard. The mechanic who taps the wheels of a railroad car is able to detect the slightest difference in tone, and is thus informed that there is a crack or flaw in the wheel. One who handles large quantities of coins will be aware of the slightest difference in the "ring" of a piece of gold or silver, that indicates that there is something wrong with the coin. A train engineer will distinguish the strange whir of something wrong with the train, amidst all the thundering rattle and roar in which it is merged. The technician in a machine shop in the same manner detects the little strange noise that indicates that something is amiss, resulting in the turning off of the power at once. Telegraphers are able to detect the almost imperceptible differences in the sound of their instruments that inform them that a new operator is on the wire; or just who is sending the message; and, in some cases, the mood or temper of the person transmitting it. Railroad and steamboat operators recognize the differences between every engine or boat on their line, or river, as the case may be. A skilled physician will detect the faint sounds denoting a respiratory trouble or a "heart murmur" in the patients. And yet these very people who are able to detect the faint differences in sound, above mentioned, are often known as "poor hearers" in other things. Why? Simply because they hear only that in which they are interested, and to which their attention has been directed. That is the whole secret, and in it is also to be found the secret of training of the ear-perception. It is all a matter of interest and attention—the details depend upon these principles.

In view of the facts just stated, it will be seen that the remedy for "poor hearing," and poor memory of things heard is to be found in the use of the will in the direction of voluntary attention and interest. So true is this that some authorities go so far as to claim that many cases of supposed slight deafness are really but the result of lack of attention and concentration on the part of the person so troubled. Often what commonly appears to be deafness is not can be attributed to this cause—the sounds being heard but not being interpreted or recognized.

Sounds may be distinctly heard when the attention is directed toward them, that in ordinary circumstances would be imperceptible People often fail to hear what is said to them because they are not paying attention There are but few persons who have not had the experience of listening to some bore, whose words were distinctly heard but the meaning of which was entirely lost because of inattention and lack of interest. In hearing we must distinguish two different points—the audible sensation as it is developed without any intellectual interference, and the conception which we form in consequence of that sensation.

The reason that many persons do not remember things that they have heard is simply because they have not *listened properly.* Poor listening is far more common than one would suppose at first. A little self-examination will reveal to you the fact that you have fallen into the bad habit of inattention. One cannot listen to everything, of course—it would not be advisable. But one should acquire the habit of either really listening or else refusing to listen at all. The compromise of careless listening brings about deplorable results, and is really the reason why so many people "can't remember" what they have heard. It is all a matter of habit. Persons who have poor memories of ear-impressions should begin to "listen" in earnest. In order to re-acquire their lost habit of proper listening, they must exercise voluntary attention and develop interest. The following suggestions may be useful in that direction.

Try to memorize words that are spoken to you in conversation—a few sentences, or even one, at a time. You will find that the effort made to fasten the sentence on your memory will result in a concentration of the attention on the words of the speaker. Do the same thing when you are listening to a preacher, actor, TV or radio commentator or lecturer. Pick out the first sentence for memorizing, and make up your mind that your memory will be as wax to receive the impression and as steel to retain it. Listen to the stray scraps of conversation that come to your ears while walking on the street, and endeavor to memorize a sentence or two, as if you were to repeat it later in the day. Listen to the stray scraps of conversation that come to your ears while walking on the street, and endeavor to memorize a sentence or two, as if you were to repeat it later in the day. You will find this most interesting and helpful. You will be surprised at the details that such analysis will reveal. Listen to the footsteps of different persons and endeavor to distinguish between them—each has its peculiarities. Get some one to read a line or two of poetry or prose to you, and then endeavor to remember it. A little practice of this kind will greatly develop the power of voluntary attention to sounds and spoken words. But above everything else, practice repeating the words and sounds that you have memorized, so far as is possible—for by so doing you will get the mind into the habit of taking an interest in sound impressions. In this way you not only improve the sense of hearing, but also the faculty of remembering.

If you will analyze, and boil down the above remarks and directions, you will find that the gist of the whole matter is that one should *actually use, employ and exercise* the mental faculty of hearing, actively and intelligently. Nature has a way of putting to sleep, or atrophying any faculty that is not used or exercised; and also of encouraging, developing and strengthening any faculty that is properly employed and exercised. In this you have the secret. Use it. If you will listen well, you will hear well and remember well that which you have heard.

Key Points

Just as it is true that it is the mind and not the eye that really *sees;* so is it true that it is the mind and not the ear that really *hears.*

The mind will hear the faintest sounds from things in which is centered interest and attention, while at the same time ignoring things in which there is no interest and to which the attention is not turned.

The remedy for poor hearing, and poor memory of things heard is to be found in the use of the will in the direction of voluntary attention and interest.

The reason that many persons do not remember things that they have heard is simply because they have not *listened properly.*

Ways to improve your listening skills:

Memorize and repeat words and thoughts heard in conversations, lectures, sermons, TV and radio programs. Pick out the first sentence for memorizing, and make up your mind that your memory will be as wax to receive the impression and as steel to retain it.

Listen to the stray scraps of conversation that come to your ears while walking on the street, and endeavor to memorize a sentence or two, as if you were to repeat it later in the day.

Listen to the footsteps of different persons and endeavor to distinguish between them—each has its peculiarities.

Get some one to read a line or two of poetry or prose to you, and then endeavor to remember it. A little practice of this kind will greatly develop the power of voluntary attention to sounds and spoken words.

Above everything else, practice repeating the words and sounds that you have memorized, so far as is possible—for by so doing you will get the mind into the habit of taking an interest in sound impressions. In this way you not only improve the sense of hearing, but also the faculty of remembering.

CHAPTER 11

HOW TO REMEMBER NAMES

The phase of memory connected with the remembrance or recollection of names probably is of greater interest to the majority of persons than are any of the associated phases of the subject. Many people are embarrassed by their failure to recall the name of some one whom they feel they know, but whose name has escaped them. This failure to remember the names of persons undoubtedly interferes with the business and professional success of many persons; and, on the other hand, the ability to recall names readily has aided many persons in the struggle for success. It would seem that there are a greater number of persons deficient in this phase of memory than in any other. The memory of names is a subject with which most persons must have a more than passing interest.

The number of persons who never or rarely forget a name is exceedingly small; the number of those who have a poor memory for them is very large. The reason for this is partly a defect of mental development and partly a matter of habit. In either case it may be overcome by effort.

You will find that the majority of successful people have been able to recall the faces and names of those with whom they came in contact, and it is an interesting subject for speculation as to just how much of their success was due to this faculty. Socrates is said to have easily remembered the names of all of his students, and his classes numbered thousands in the course of a year. It has been said of Washington and Napoleon that they knew the names of every one of their soldiers. The Roman Emperor, Trajan, is said to have known the names of all the Praetorian Guards, numbering about 12,000. Pericles knew the face and name of every one of the citizens of Athens. John Wesley could recall the names of thousands of persons whom he had met in his travels. Henry Clay was specially developed in this phase of memory, and there was a tradition among his followers that he remembered every one whom he met.

There have been many theories advanced, and explanations offered to account for the fact that the recollection of names is far more difficult than any other form of the activities of the memory. The difficulty in the recollection of names is caused by the fact that names in themselves are *uninteresting* and therefore do not attract or hold the attention, as do other objects presented to the mind. Sound impressions are apt to be more difficult of recollection than sight impressions, but the lack of interesting qualities in names is believed to be the principal obstacle and difficulty. Names by themselves do not usually conjure up a mental picture. Common nouns, often are identified with some object having shape, or appearance which can be *seen or imagined:* in other words *a mental image* of it can be formed. This is not true of names by themselves unless the *name* can be associated with a mental image,

But in spite of this difficulty, persons have and can greatly improve their memory of names. Many who were originally very deficient in this respect have not only improved the faculty far beyond its former condition, but have also developed exceptional ability in this special phase of memory so that they became noted for their unfailing recollection of the names of those with whom they came in contact.

Perhaps the best *way* to express the various methods that may be used for this purpose would be to relate the actual experience of an employee of a bank in one of the large cities of this country, who made a close study of the subject and developed this skill far beyond the ordinary. Starting with a remarkably poor memory for names, he became known to his associates as "the man who never forgets a name." His first step was to take a number of "courses" in secret "methods" of developing the memory; but after spending much money he expressed his disgust with the whole idea of artificial memory training. He then started in to study the subject from the point-of-view of The New Psychology, putting into effect all of the tested principles, and improving upon some of their details.

The man, whom we shall call "Mr. X.," decided that the first thing for him to do was to develop his faculty of receiving clear and distinct sound impressions. In doing this he followed the plan outlined in the chapter on "Training the

Ear." He persevered and practiced along these lines until his "hearing" became very acute. He made a study of voices, until he could classify them and analyze their characteristics. Then he found that he could *hear* names in a manner before impossible to him. That is, instead of merely catching a vague sound of a name, he would hear it so clearly and distinctly that a firm registration would be obtained on the records of his memory. For the first time in his life names began to *mean something* to him. He paid attention to every name he heard, just as he did to every note he handled. He would repeat a name to himself, after hearing it, and would thus strengthen the impression. If he came across an unusual name, he would write it down several times, at the first opportunity, thus obtaining the benefit of a double sense impression, adding eye impression to ear impression. All this, of course, aroused his interest in the subject of names in general, which led him to the next step in his progress.

Mr. X. then began to study names, their origin, their peculiarities, their differences, points of resemblances, etc. He made a hobby of names, and evinced all the joy of a collector when he was able to stick the pin of attention through the specimen of a new and unfamiliar species of name. He began to collect names, just as others collect beetles, stamps, coins, etc., and took quite a pride in his collection and in his knowledge of the subject. He read books on names, from the libraries, giving their origin, etc. He had a special delight in "queer" names, and would amuse his friends by relating the funny names he had seen on signs, and otherwise. He took a small City Directory home with him, and would run over the pages in the evening, looking up new names, and classifying old ones into groups. He found that some names were derived from animals, and put these into a class by themselves—the Lyons, Wolfs, Foxes, Lambs, Hares, etc. Others were put into the color group—Blacks, Greens, Whites, Greys, Blues, etc. Others belonged to the bird family—Crows, Hawks, Birds, Drakes, Cranes, Doves, Jays, etc. Others belonged to trades—Millers, Smiths, Coopers, Carpenters, Bakers, Painters, etc. Others were trees—Chestnuts, Oakleys, Walnuts, Cherrys, Pines, etc. Then there were Hills and Dales; Fields and Mountains; Lanes and Brooks. Some were Strong; others were Gay; others were Savage; others Noble. And so on. It would take a whole book to tell you what that man found out about names. He came near becoming a "crank" on the subject. But his hobby began to manifest excellent results, for his *interest* had been awakened to an unusual degree, and he was becoming very proficient in his recollection of names, for they now meant something to him. He easily recalled all the regular customers at his bank—quite a number by the way for the bank was a large one—and many occasional depositors were delighted to have themselves called by name by our friend. Occasionally he would meet with a name that balked him, in which case he would repeat it over to himself, and write it a number of times until he had mastered it—after that it never escaped him.

Mr. X. would always repeat a name when it was spoken, and would at the look intently at the person bearing it, thus seeming to fix the two together in his mind at the same-time—when he wanted them they would be found in each other's company. He also acquired the habit of *visualizing* the name—that is, he would see its letters in his mind's eye, as a picture. This he regarded as a most important point, and we thoroughly agree with him. He used the Law of Association in the direction of associating a new man with a well-remembered man of the same name. A new Mr. Schmidtzenberger would be associated with an old customer of the same name—when he would see the new man, he would think of the old one, and the name would flash into his mind. To sum up the whole method, however, it may be said that the gist of the thing was in *taking an interest* in names in general. In this way an uninteresting subject was made interesting—and we always have a good memory for the things in which we are interested.

The case of Mr. X. is an extreme one—and the results obtained were beyond the ordinary. You may obtain the same results in the degree that you work for it. Make a study of names—start a collection—and you will have no trouble in developing a memory for them. This is the whole thing in a nutshell.

Key Points

The number of persons who never or rarely forget a name is exceedingly small; the number of those who have a poor memory for them is very large. The reason for this is partly a defect of mental development and partly a matter of habit. In either case it may be overcome by effort.

The difficulty in the recollection of names is caused by the fact that names in themselves are *uninteresting* and therefore do not attract or hold the attention, as do other objects presented to the mind. Sound impressions are apt to be more difficult of recollection than sight impressions, but the lack of interesting qualities in names is believed to be the principal obstacle and difficulty.

Suggestions on improving memory of names:

Make a study of names—start a collection—and you will have no trouble in developing a memory for them.

Listen carefully to the name, Instead of merely catching a vague sound of a name, listen to it so clearly and distinctly that a firm registration is obtained on the records of you memory.

Repeat the name after hearing it to strengthen the impression. If it is an unusual name, write it down several times, at the first opportunity, thus obtaining the benefit of a double sense impression, adding eye impression to ear impression.

CHAPTER 12
HOW TO REMEMBER FACES

The memory of faces is closely connected with the memory of names, and yet the two are not always associated, for there are many people who easily remember faces, and yet forget names, and vice versa. In some ways, however, the memory of faces is a necessary precedent for the recollection of the names of people. Unless we recall the face, we are unable to make the necessary association with the name of the person. We have given a number of instances of face-memory, in the preceding chapter. This chapter, will concentrate on the subject of the recollection of the features of persons, irrespective of their names.

This faculty is possessed by all persons, but in varying degrees. Those in whom it is well developed seem to recognize the faces of persons whom they have met years before, and to associate them with the circumstances in which they last met them, even where the name escapes the memory.

Others seem to forget a face the moment it passes from view, and fail to recognize the same persons whom they met only a few hours before, much to their mortification and chagrin.

Detectives, newspaper reporters, and others who come in contact with many people, usually have this faculty largely developed, for it becomes a necessity of their work, and their interest and attention is rendered active thereby. Public men often have this faculty largely developed by reason of the necessities of their life. It is said that Jim Farley, the political leader who propelled Franklin D. Roosevelt to the White House, never forgot the face of anyone whom he had met and conversed with a few moments. This faculty rendered him very popular in political life. In this respect he resembled Henry Clay, who was noted for his memory of faces. It is related of Clay that he once paid a visit of a few hours to a small town in Mississippi, on an electioneering tour. Amidst the throng surrounding him was an old man, with one eye missing. The old fellow pressed forward crying out that he was sure that Henry Clay would remember him. Clay took a sharp look at him and said: "I met you in Kentucky many years ago, did I not?" "Yes," replied the man. "Did you lose your eye since then?" asked Clay. "Yes, several years after," replied the old man. "Turn your face side-ways, so that I can see your profile," said Clay. The man did so. Then Clay smiled, triumphantly, saying: "I've got you now— weren't you on that jury in the Innes case at Frankfort, that I tried in the United States Court over twenty years ago?" "Yes siree!" said the man, "I knowed that ye know me, 'n I told 'em you would." And the crowd gave a whoop, and Clay knew that he was safe in that town and county.

Vidocq, the celebrated French detective, is said to have never forgotten a face of a criminal whom he had once seen. A celebrated instance of this power on his part is that of the case of Delafranche, the forger who escaped from prison and dwelt in foreign lands for over twenty years. After that time he returned to Paris feeling secure from detection, because he had become bald, lost an eye, and his nose had become badly mutilated. Moreover he disguised himself and wore a beard, in order to still further evade detection. One day Vidocq met him on the street, and recognized him at once, resulting in his arrest and return to prison. Instances of this kind could be multiplied indefinitely.

The way to develop this phase of memory is akin to that urged in the development of other phases—the cultivation of interest, and the bestowal of attention. Faces as a whole are not apt to prove interesting. It is only by analyzing and classifying them that the study begins to grow of interest to us. The study of a good elementary work on physiognomy is recommended to those wishing to develop the faculty of remembering faces, for in such a work the student is led to notice the different kinds of noses, ears, eyes, chins, foreheads, etc., such notice and recognition tending to induce an interest in this area. A rudimentary course of study in drawing faces, particularly in profile, will also tend to make one "take notice" and will awaken interest. If you are required to draw a nose, particularly from memory, you will be apt to give to it your interested attention. The matter of interest is vital. If you were shown a man and told that the next time you met and recognized him he would hand you over $500, you would be very apt to study his face carefully, and to recognize him later on; whereas the same man if introduced casually as a "Mr. Jones," would arouse no interest and the chances of recognition would be slim.

Every time we enter a public place we see different types of people, and there is a great deal to be noticed about each type. Every human countenance shows its past history to one who knows how to look. Successful gamblers often become so expert in noticing the slightest change of an opponent's facial expression that they will estimate the strength of his or her hand by the involuntary signs which appear in the face and which are frequently checked the instant they appear.

Of all classes, perhaps artists are more apt to form a clear-cut image of the features of persons whom they meet— particularly if they are portrait painters. There are instances of celebrated portrait painters who were able to execute a good portrait after having once carefully studied the face of the sitter, their memory enabling them to visualize the features at will. Some celebrated teachers of drawing have instructed their scholars to take a sharp hasty glance at a nose, an eye, an ear, or chin, and then to so clearly visualize it that they could draw it perfectly. It is all a matter of interest, attention, and practice. This is a faculty that is of importance in all technical and artistic occupations. It gives accuracy to our perceptions, and justice to our generalizations; however, it is starved by lazy disuse. Instead of being cultivated judiciously in such a way that will, on the whole, bring the best return.

The celebrated painter Leonardo da Vinci invented a most ingenious method for identifying faces, and by it is said to have been able to reproduce from memory any face that he had once carefully scrutinized. He drew all the possible forms of the nose, mouth, chin, eyes, ears and forehead, numbered them 1, 2, 3, 4, etc., and committed them thoroughly to memory. Then, whenever he saw a face that he wished to draw or paint from memory, he noted in his mind that it was chin 4, eyes 2, nose 5, ears 6—or whatever the combinations might be—and by retaining the analysis in his memory he could reconstruct the face at any time. This may be too complex for the average person, yet a modification of it would prove useful. That is, if you would begin to form a classification of several kinds of noses, such as straight, crooked, pug and all the other varieties, you would soon recognize noses when you saw them. And the same with mouths, a few classes being found to cover the majority of cases.

But of all the features, the eye is the most expressive, and the one most easily remembered, when clearly noticed. Detectives rely much upon *the expression of the eye.* If you ever fully catch the *expression* of a person's eye, you will be very apt to recognize it thereafter. Therefore concentrate on eyes in studying faces.

A good plan in developing this faculty is to visualize the faces of persons you have met during the day, in the evening. Try to develop the faculty of visualizing the features of those whom you know—this will start you off right. Draw them in your mind—see them with your mind's eye, until you can visualize the features of very old friends; then do the same with acquaintances, and so on, until you are able to visualize the features of every one you "know." Then start on to add to your list by recalling in the imagination, the features of strangers whom you meet. By a little practice of this kind you will develop a great interest in faces and your memory of them, and the power to recall them will increase rapidly. The secret is to study faces—to be interested in them. In this way you add zest to the task, and make a pleasure of drudgery. The study of photographs is also a great aid in this work—but study them in detail, not as a whole. If you can arouse sufficient interest in features and faces, you will have no trouble in remembering and recalling them. The two things go together.

Key Points

The ability to remember faces is possessed by all persons, but in varying degrees. Those in whom it is well developed seem to recognize the faces of persons whom they have met years before, and to associate them with the circumstances in which they last met them, even where the name escapes the memory. Others seem to forget a face the moment it passes from view, and fail to recognize the same persons whom they met only a few hours before.

The study of a good elementary work on physiognomy is recommended to those wishing to develop the faculty of remembering faces, for in such a work the student is led to notice the different kinds of noses, ears, eyes, chins, foreheads, etc., such notice and recognition tending to induce an interest in the subject of features.

A good plan in developing this faculty is to visualize the faces of persons you have met during the day, in the evening. Try to develop the faculty of visualizing the features of those whom you know—this will start you off right. Draw them in your mind—see them with your mind's eye, until you can visualize the features of very old friends; then do the same with acquaintances, and so on, until you are able to visualize the features of every one you "know." Then start on to add to your list by recalling in the imagination, the features of strangers whom you meet. By a little practice of this kind you will develop a great interest in faces and your memory of them, and the power to recall them will increase rapidly.

CHAPTER 13
HOW TO REMEMBER PLACES

There is a great difference in the various degrees of development of "the sense of locality" in different persons. But these differences may be traced directly to the degree of memory of that particular phase or faculty of the mind, which in turn depends upon the degree of attention, interest, and use that has been bestowed upon the faculty in question. The faculty of locality includes cognizance of place; recollection of the looks of places, roads, scenery, and the location of objects; where on a page ideas are to be found, and position generally; the geographical faculty; the desire to see places, and have the ability to find them.

Persons in whom this faculty is developed to the highest degree seem to have an almost intuitive idea of direction, place and position. They never get lost or "mixed up" regarding direction or place. They remember the places they visit and their relation in space to each other. Their minds are like maps upon which are engraved the various roads, streets and objects of sight in every direction. When these people think of China, Labrador, Terra del Fuego, Norway, Cape of Good Hope, Tibet, or any other place, they seem to think of it in *"this* direction or *that* direction" rather than as a vague place situated in a vague direction. Their minds think "north, south, east or west" as the case may be when they consider a given place. Shading down by degrees we find people at the other pole of the faculty who seem to find it impossible to remember any direction, or locality or relation in space. Such people are constantly losing themselves in their own towns, and fear to trust themselves in a strange place. They have no sense of direction, or place, and fail to recognize a street or scene that they have visited recently, not to speak of those that they traveled over in time past. Between these two poles or degrees there is a vast difference, and it is difficult to realize that it is all a matter of use, interest and attention. That it is but this may be proven by anyone who will take the trouble and pains to develop the faculty and memory of locality within his mind. Many have done this, and anyone else may do likewise if the proper methods were employed.

The secret of the development of the faculty and memory of place and locality is akin to that mentioned in the preceding chapters, in connection with the development of the memory for names and faces. The first thing necessary is to develop an interest in the subject. You should begin to "take notice" of the direction of the streets or roads over which you travel; the landmarks; the turns of the road; the natural objects along the way. You should study maps, until you awaken a new interest in them, just as did Mr. X, who used the directory in order to take an interest in names. You should procure a small geography book and study direction, distances, location, shape and form of countries, etc., not as a mere mechanical thing but as a live subject of interest. If there were a large sum of money awaiting your coming in certain sections of the globe, you would manifest a decided interest in the direction, locality and position of those places, and the best way to reach them. Before long you would be a veritable reference book regarding those special places. The whole thing lies in the degree of "want to" regarding the matter. Desire awakens interest; interest employs attention; and attention brings use. You must first want to develop the faculty of locality—and want to "hard enough." The rest is a mere matter of detail.

One of the first things to do, after arousing an interest, is to carefully note the landmarks and relative positions of the streets or roads over which you travel. So many people travel along a new street or road in an absent-minded manner, taking no notice of the lay of the land as they proceed. This is fatal to place-memory. You must take notice of the thoroughfares and the things along the way. Pause at the cross roads, or the street-corners and note the landmarks, and the general directions and relative positions, until they are firmly imprinted on your mind. Begin to see how many things you can remember regarding even a little exercise walk. And when you have returned home, go over the trip in your mind, and see how much of the direction and how many of the landmarks you are able to remember. Take out your pencil, and endeavor to *make a map of* your route, giving the general directions, and noting the street names, and principal objects of interest. Fix the idea of "North" in your mind when starting, and keep your bearings by it during your whole trip, and in your map-making. You will be surprised how much interest you will soon develop in this map-making. It will get to be quite a game, and you will experience pleasure in your increasing proficiency in it. When you go out for a walk or a drive in your car, go in a round-about way, taking as many turns and twists as possible, in order to exercise your faculty of locality and direction—but always note carefully direction and general course, so that you may reproduce it correctly on your map when you return. If you have a city map, compare it with your own little map, and also retrace your route, in imagination, on the map. With a city map or road map, you may get lots of amusement by re-traveling the route of your little journeys.

Always note the names of the various streets over which you travel, as well as those that you cross during your walk or ride. Note them down upon your map, and you will find that you will develop a rapidly improving memory in this direction—because you have awakened interest and bestowed attention. Take a pride in your map making. If you have a companion, endeavor to beat each other at this game—both traveling over the same route together, and then seeing which one can remember the greatest number of details of the journey.

Akin to this, and supplementary to it, is the plan of selecting a route to be traveled, on your city map, endeavoring to fix in your mind the general directions, names of streets, turns, return journey, etc., before you start. Begin by mapping out a short trip in this way, and then increase it every day. After mapping out a trip, lay aside your map and travel it in person. If you like, take along the map and from time to time puzzle out variations. Get the map habit in every possible variation and form, but do not depend upon the map exclusively; but instead, endeavor to correlate the printed map with the mental map that you are building in your brain.

If you are about to take a journey to a strange place, study your maps carefully before you go, and exercise your memory by reproducing them with a pencil. Then as you travel along, compare places with your map, and you will find that you will take an entirely new interest in the trip—it will begin by meaning something to you. If about to visit a strange city, procure a map of it before starting, and begin by noting the cardinal points of the compass, study the map—the directions of the principal streets and the relative positions of the principal points of interest, buildings, etc. In this way you not only develop your memory of places, and render yourself proof against being lost, but you also provide a source of new and great interest in your visit.

The above suggestions are capable of the greatest expansion and variation on the part of anyone who practices them. The whole thing depends upon the "taking notice" and using the attention, and those things in turn depend upon the taking of interest in the subject. If you will "wake up and take interest" in the subject of locality and direction you may develop yourself along the lines of place-memory to an almost incredible degree, in a comparatively short time.

There is no other phase of memory that so quickly responds to use and exercise as this one. For example, Mrs. G., was notoriously deficient in the memory of place, and was sure to lose herself a few blocks from her stopping place, wherever she might be. She seemed absolutely devoid of the sense of direction or locality and often lost herself in the hotel corridors, notwithstanding the fact that for years she traveled all over the world with her husband. The trouble undoubtedly arose from the fact that she depended altogether upon her husband as a pilot, the couple being inseparable. After Mr. G. died the lady lost her pilot. Instead of giving up in despair, she began to rise to the occasion— having no pilot, she had to pilot herself. She was forced to "wake up and take notice." For the next couple of years, she had to travel extensively to close up certain business matters of her husband's. In order to get around safely, she was forced to take an interest in where she was going. Before the two years' travels were over, she was as good a traveler as her husband had ever been, and was frequently called upon as a guide by others in whose company she chanced to be. She explained it by saying "Why, I don't know just how I did it—I just *had to,* that's all—I just *did* it." What Mrs. G "just did," was accomplished by an instinctive following of the plan recommended in the preceding paragraphs. She "just *had to*" use maps and to "take notice."

So true are the principles underlying this method of developing the place-memory, that those deficient in it, providing they will arouse intense interest and will stick to it, may develop the faculty to such an extent that they may almost rival the cat which "always came back," or the dog which "you couldn't lose." The Indians, Bedouins, Gypsies and other people of the plains, forest, desert, and mountains, have this faculty so highly developed that it seems almost like an extra sense. It is all this matter of "taking notice" sharpened by continuous need, use and exercise, to a high degree. The mind will respond to the need if people like Mrs. G. are compelled to do it. The laws of Attention and Association will work wonders when actively called into play by interest or need, followed by exercise and use. There is no magic in the process—just "want to" and "keep at it," that's all. Do you want to hard enough—have you the determination to keep at it?

Key Points

The faculty of locality includes cognizance of place; recollection of the looks of places, roads, scenery, and the location of objects; where on a page ideas are to be found, and position generally; the geographical faculty; the desire to see places, and have the ability to find them.

Procure a small geography book and study direction, distances, location, shape and form of countries, etc., not as a mere mechanical thing but as a live subject of interest

When you go out for a walk or a drive in your car, go in a round-about way, taking as many turns and twists as possible, in order to exercise your faculty of locality and direction—but always note carefully direction and general course, so that you may reproduce it correctly on your map when you return.

If about to visit a strange city, procure a map of it before starting, and begin by noting the cardinal points of the compass, study the map—the directions of the principal streets and the relative positions of the principal points of interest, buildings, etc. In this way you not only develop your memory of places, and render yourself proof against being lost, but you also provide a source of new and great interest in your visit.

CHAPTER 14
HOW TO REMEMBER NUMBERS

The faculty of knowing, recognizing and remembering figures in the abstract and in their relation to each other, differs very materially among different individuals. To some, figures and numbers are apprehended and remembered with ease, while to others they possess no interest, attraction or affinity, and consequently are not apt to be remembered. It is generally admitted by the best authorities that the memorizing of dates, figures, numbers, etc., is the most difficult of any of the phases of memory. But all agree that the faculty may be developed by practice and interest. There have been instances of persons having this faculty of the mind developed to a degree almost incredible; and other instances of persons having started with an aversion to figures and then developing an interest which resulted in their acquiring a remarkable degree of proficiency along these lines.

Many of the celebrated mathematicians and astronomers developed wonderful memories for figures. Sir William Herschel, the British astronomer, who discovered the planet Uranus, is said to have been able to remember all the details of intricate calculations in his astronomical computations, even to the figures of the fractions. It is said that he was able to perform the most intricate calculations mentally, without the use of pen or pencil, and then dictated to his assistant the entire details of the process, including the final results.

Tycho Brahe, the sixteenth century Danish astronomer, also possessed a similar memory. It is said that he rebelled at being compelled to refer to the printed tables of square roots and cube roots, and in a half day, memorize the entire set of tables, an almost incredible task that required the memorizing of over 75,000 figures, and their relations to each other. Leonhard Euler, the eighteenth century Swiss mathematician became blind in his old age, and being unable to refer to his tables, memorized them. It is said that he was able to repeat from recollection the first six powers of all the numbers from one to one hundred.

Another astounding feat of memory is that a cashier of a Chicago bank, who was able to mentally restore the accounts of the bank, which had been destroyed in the great fire in that city. His account was found to agree perfectly with the other memoranda in the case, the work performed by him being solely the work of his memory.

The mathematical prodigy, Zerah Colburn, who lived in the early nineteenth century, was perhaps the most remarkable of any of these remarkable people. In his early childhood he began to develop the most amazing qualities of mind regarding figures. He was able to instantly make the mental calculation of the exact number of seconds or minutes there was in a given time. On one occasion, when asked to calculate the number of minutes and seconds contained in forty-eight years, he gave the answer: "25,228,800 minutes, and 1,513,728,000 seconds" almost instantaneously. He could instantly multiply any number of one to three figures, by another number consisting of the same number of figures; the factors of any number consisting of six or seven figures; the square, and cube roots, and the prime numbers of any numbers given him. He mentally raised the number 8, progressively, to its sixteenth power, the result being 281,474,976,710,656; and gave the square root of 106,929, which was 5. He mentally extracted the cube root of 268,336,125; and the squares of 244,999,755 and 1,224,998,755. In five seconds he calculated the cube root of 413,993,348,677. He found the factors of 4,294,967,297, which had previously been considered to be a prime number. He mentally calculated the square of 999,999, which is 999,998,000,001 and then multiplied that number by 49, and the product by the same number, and the whole by 25—the latter as extra measure.

The great difficulty in remembering numbers, to the majority of persons, is the fact that numbers "do not mean anything to them"—that is, that numbers are thought of only in their abstract phase and nature, and are consequently far more difficult to remember than are impressions received from the senses of sight or sound. The remedy, however, becomes apparent when we recognize the source of the difficulty. The remedy is: *Make the number the subject of sound and sight impressions.* Attach the abstract idea of the numbers to the sense of impressions of sight or sound, or both, according to which are the best developed in your particular case.

It may be difficult for you to remember "1848" as an abstract thing, but comparatively easy for you to remember the *sound* of "eighteen forty-eight," or the *shape and appearance* of "1848." If you will repeat a number to yourself, so that you grasp the sound impression *of* it, or else visualize it so that you can remember having *seen* it—then you will be far more apt to remember it than if you merely think of it without reference to sound or form. You may forget that the number of a certain store or house is 3948, but you may easily remember the sound of the spoken words "thirty-nine forty-eight," or the form of "3948" as it appeared to your sight on the door of the place. In the latter case, you associate the number with the door and when you visualize the door you visualize the number.

"Children accustomed to calculate in their heads write mentally with chalk on an imaginary board the figures in question, then all their partial operations, then the final sum, so that they see internally the different lines of white figures with which they are concerned. A young man, who had never been at school and did not know how to read or write, said that, when making his calculations he saw them clearly before him. Another said that he saw the numbers he was working with as if they had been written on a chalk-board. He added: "If I perform a sum mentally, it always proceeds in a visible form in my mind; indeed, I can conceive of no other way possible of doing mental arithmetic."

There are people who could never remember the number of an address until it was distinctly repeated to them several times—then they memorized the *sound and* never forget it. Others forget the sounds, or failed to register them in the mind, but after once seeing the number on the door of an office or store, could repeat it at a moments notice, saying that they mentally "could see the figures on the door." You will find by a little questioning that the majority of people remember figures or numbers in this way, and that very few can remember them as abstract things. For that matter it is difficult for the majority of persons to even think of a number, abstractly. Try it yourself, and ascertain whether you do not remember the number as either *a sound of words,* or else as the mental image or visualization of the *form of the figures.* And, by the way, which ever it happens to be, sight or sound, that particular kind of remembrance is *your* best way of remembering numbers, and consequently gives you the lines upon which you should proceed to develop this phase of memory.

The law of Association may be used advantageously in memorizing numbers; for instance one person reported that she remembered the number 186,000 (the number of miles per second traveled by light-waves in the atmosphere) by associating it with the number of her father's former place of business, "186." Another remembered his telephone number "1776" by recalling the date of the Declaration of Independence.

But by far the better way to memorize dates, special numbers connected with events, etc., is to visualize the picture of the event with the picture of the date or number, thus combining the two things into a mental picture, the association of which will be preserved when the picture is recalled. Verse of doggerel, such as "In fourteen hundred and ninety-two, Columbus sailed the ocean blue;" or "In eighteen hundred and sixty-one, our country's Civil war begun," etc., have their places and uses. But it is far better to cultivate the "sight or sound" of a number, than to depend upon cumbersome associative methods based on artificial links and pegs.

Before you can develop a good memory of a subject, you must first cultivate an interest in that subject. Therefore, if you will keep your interest in figures alive by working out a few problems in mathematics, once in a while, you will find that figures will begin to have a new interest for you. A little elementary arithmetic, used with interest, will do more to start you on the road to "How to Remember Numbers" than a dozen textbooks on the subject.

In memory, the three rules are: "Interest, Attention and Exercise"—and the last is the most important, for without it the others fail. You will be surprised to see how many interesting things there are in figures, as you proceed. The task of going over the elementary arithmetic will not be nearly so "dry" as when you were a child. You will uncover all sorts of "queer" things in relation to numbers. Just as a "sample" let us call your attention to a few:

Take the figure "1" and place behind it a number of zeros, thus 1,000,000,000,000—as many zeros as you wish. Then divide the number by the figure "7." You will find that the result is always this "142,857" then another "142,857," and so on to infinity. These six figures will be repeated over and over again. Then multiply this "142,857" by the figure "7," and your product will be *all nines.* Then take any number, and set it down, placing beneath it a reversal of itself and subtract the latter from the former, thus:

$$117,761,909$$
$$-90,916,771$$
$$26,845,138$$

and you will find that the result will always reduce to nine, and is always a multiple of 9. Take any number composed of two or more figures, and subtract from it the added sum of its separate figures, and the result is always a multiple of 9, thus :

184 [1+8+4 = 13]
184 – 13 = 171 (which is 19, a multiple of 9)

These examples are presented to remind you that there is much more of interest in mere figures than many would suppose. If you can arouse your interest in them, then you will be well started on the road to the memorizing of numbers. Let figures and numbers "mean something" to you, and the rest will be merely a matter of detail.

Key Points

The great difficulty in remembering numbers, to the majority of persons, is the fact that numbers "do not mean anything to them"—that is, that numbers are thought of only in their abstract phase and nature, and are consequently far more difficult to remember than are impressions received from the senses of sight or sound. The remedy, however, becomes apparent when we recognize the source of the difficulty. The remedy is: *Make the number the subject of sound and sight impressions.* Attach the abstract idea of the numbers to the sense of impressions of sight or sound, or both, according to which are the best developed in your particular case.

A good way to memorize dates, special numbers connected with events, etc., is to visualize the picture of the event with the picture of the date or number, thus combining the two things into a mental picture, the association of which will be preserved when the picture is recalled.

In memory, the three rules are: "Interest, Attention and Exercise"—and the last is the most important, for without it the others fail.

Let figures and numbers "mean something" to you, and the rest will be merely a matter of detail.

CHAPTER 15
HOW TO REMEMBER MUSIC

Like all of the other faculties of the mind, different individuals manifest that of music or tune in varying degrees. To some music seems to be almost instinctively grasped, while to others it is acquired only by great effort and much labor. To some harmony is natural, and lack of harmony a matter of repulsion, while others fail to recognize the difference between the two except in extreme cases. Some seem to be the very soul of music, while others have no conception of what the soul of music may be. Then there is manifested the different phases of the knowledge of music. Some play correctly by ear, but are clumsy and inefficient when it comes to playing by note. Others play very correctly in a mechanical manner, but fail to retain the memory of music that they have heard. It is indeed a good musician who combines within himself or herself, both of the two last mentioned faculties—the ear perception of music and the ability to execute correctly from notes.

There are many cases of record in which extraordinary powers of memory of music have been manifested. A great Irish bard once met a noted musician and challenged him to a test of their respective musical abilities. The *challenge was* accepted and the musician played on his violin one of Vivaldi's most difficult concertos. On the conclusion of the performance, the bard, who had never heard the piece before, took his harp and played the concerto through from beginning to end without making a single error.

Beethoven could retain in his memory any musical composition, however complex, that he had listened to, and could reproduce most of it. He could play from memory every one of the compositions in Bach's 'Well Tempered Clavichord,' there being forty-eight preludes and the same number of fugues, which in intricacy of movement and difficulty of execution are almost unexampled, as each of these compositions is written in the most abstruse style of counterpoint.

Mozart, at four years of age, could remember note for note, elaborate solos in concertos, which he had heard; he could learn a minuet in half an hour, and even composed short pieces at that early age. At six he was able to compose without the aid of an instrument, and continued to advance rapidly in musical memory and knowledge. When fourteen years old he went to Rome in Holy Week. At the Sistine Chapel Allegri's 'Miserere,' was performed each day, the score of which Mozart wished to obtain, but he learned that no copies were allowed to be made. He listened attentively to the performance, at the conclusion of which he wrote the whole score from memory without an error. Another time, Mozart was engaged to contribute an original composition to be performed by a noted violinist and himself at Vienna before the Emperor Joseph. On arriving at the appointed place Mozart discovered that he had forgotten to bring his part. Nothing dismayed, he placed a blank sheet of paper before him, and played his part through from memory without a mistake.

When the opera of 'Don Giovanni' was first performed there was no time to copy the score for the harpsichord, but Mozart was equal to the occasion; he conducted the entire opera and played the harpsichord accompaniment to the songs and choruses without a note before him.

There are many well-attested instances of Mendelssohn's remarkable musical memory. He once gave a grand concert in London, at which his Overture to 'Midsummer Night's Dream' was produced. There was only one copy of the full score, which was taken charge of by the organist of St. Paul's Cathedral, who unfortunately left it in a hackney coach—whereupon Mendelssohn wrote out another score from memory, without an error.

At another time, when about to direct a public performance of Bach's 'Passion Music,' he found on mounting the conductor's platform that instead of the score of the work to be performed, that of another composition had been brought by mistake. Without hesitation Mendelssohn successfully conducted this complicated work from memory, automatically turning over leaf after leaf of the score before him as the performance progressed, so that no feeling of uneasiness might enter the minds of the orchestra and singers. The American composer, Louis M. Gottschalk, could play from memory several thousand compositions, including many of the works of Bach. There are many examples of famous conductors, who have conducted every note of many operas from memory.

It will be seen that two phases of memory must enter into the "memory of music"—the memory of tune and the memory of the notes. The memory of tune of course falls into the class of ear-impressions, and what has been said regarding them is also applicable to this case. The memory of notes falls into the classification of eye-impressions, and the rules of this class of memory applies in this ease. As to the cultivation of the memory of tune, the principle advice to be given is to take an active interest in all that pertains to the sound of music, and also take every opportunity for listening to good music, and endeavoring to reproduce it in the imagination or memory. Endeavor to enter into the spirit of the music until it becomes a part of you. Do not be content with merely hearing it, but lend yourself to a *feeling* of its meaning. The more the music "means to you," the more easily you will remember it.

The plan followed by many students—particularly those of vocal music, is to have a few bars of a piece played over to them several times, until they are able to hum it correctly; then a few more are added; and then a few more and so on. Each addition must be reviewed in connection with that which was learned before, so that the chain of association may be kept unbroken. The principle is the same as the child learning the A-B-C's—"B" is remembered because it follows "A." By this constant addition of "just a little bit more," accompanied by frequent reviews, long and difficult pieces may be memorized.

The memory of notes may be developed by the method above named—the method of learning a few bars well, and then adding a few more, and frequently reviewing as far as you have learned, forging the links of association as you go along, by frequent practice. The method being entirely that of eye-impression and subject to its rules, you must observe the idea of visualization—that is learning each bar until you can *see* it "in your mind's eye" as you proceed.

But in this, as in many other eye-impressions, you will find that you will be greatly aided by your memory of the *sound* of the notes, in addition to their appearance. Try to associate the two as much as possible, so that when you *see,* a note, you will *hear* the sound of it, and when you *hear a* note sounded, you will *see* it as it appears on the score. This combining of the impressions of both sight and sound will give you the benefit of the double sense impression, which results in doubling your memory efficiency. In addition to visualizing the notes themselves, add the appearance of the various symbols denoting the key, the time, the movement, expression, etc., so that you may hum the air from the visualized notes, with expression and with correct interpretation. Changes of key, time or movement should be carefully noted in the memorization of the notes. And above everything else, memorize the *feeling* of that particular portion of the score, that you may not only see and hear, but also *feel* that which you are recalling.

Practice memorizing simple songs at first. One reason is that these songs lend themselves readily to memorizing, and the chain of easy association is usually maintained throughout.

In this phase of memory, as in all others, take interest; bestow Attention; and Practice and Exercise as often as possible. You may have tired of these words—but they constitute the main principles of the development of a retentive memory. Things must be impressed upon the memory, before they may be recalled. This should be remembered in every consideration of the subject.

Key Points

There are two phases of memory essential in the "memory of music"—the memory of tune and the memory of the notes. The memory of tune of course falls into the class of ear-impressions, and what has been said regarding them is also applicable to this case. The memory of notes falls into the classification of eye-impressions, and the rules of this class of memory applies in this ease.

As to the cultivation of the memory of tune, the principle advice to be given is to take an active interest in all that pertains to the sound of music, and also take every opportunity for listening to good music, and endeavoring to reproduce it in the imagination or memory. Endeavor to enter into the spirit of the music until it becomes a part of you. Do not be content with merely hearing it, but lend yourself to a *feeling* of its meaning. The more the music "means to you," the more easily will you remember it.

Try to associate sound and vision as much as possible, so that when you *see,* a note, you will *hear* the sound of it, and when you *hear* a note sounded, you will *see* it as it appears on the score. This combining of the impressions of both sight and sound will give you the benefit of the double sense impression, which results in doubling your memory efficiency.

CHAPTER 16
HOW TO REMEMBER OCCURRENCES

The phase of memory that manifests in the recording of and recollection of the occurrences and details of one's every-day life is far more important than would appear at first thought. Most people are under the impression that they remember very well the occurrences of their every-day business, professional or social life, and is apt to be surprised to have it suggested that they really remember very little of what happens. In order to prove how very little of this kind is really remembered, lay down this book, at this place, and then quiet your mind endeavor to recall the incidents of the same day of the preceding week. You will be surprised to see how very little of what happened on that day you are really capable of recollecting. Then try the same experiment with the occurrences of yesterday—this result will also excite surprise. It is true that if you are reminded of some particular occurrence, you will recall it, more or less distinctly, but beyond that you will remember nothing. Imagine that you are called upon to testify in court, regarding the happenings of the previous day, or the day of the week before, and you will realize your position.

The reason for the failure to easily remember the events referred to is that you made no effort at the time to impress these happenings upon your subconscious mentality. You allowed them to pass from your attention. You did not wish to be bothered with the recollection of trifles, and in endeavoring to escape from them, you made the mistake of failing to store them away. There is a vast difference between dwelling on the past, and storing away past records for possible future reference. To allow the records of each day to be destroyed is like tearing up the important business papers in an *office* in order to avoid giving them a little space in the files.

It is not advisable to expend much mental effort in fastening each important detail of the day upon the mind, as it occurs; but there is an easier way that will accomplish the purpose, if one will but take a little trouble in that direction. This is the practice of *reviewing* the occurrences of each day, after the active work of the day is over. If, every evening, you will review mentally all of the occurrences of each day, you will find that the act of reviewing will employ the attention to such an extent as to register the happenings in such a manner that they will be available if ever needed thereafter. It is akin to the filing of the business papers of the day, for possible future reference. Besides this advantage, these reviews will serve you well as a reminder of many little things of immediate importance that have escaped your recollection by reason of something that followed them in the field of attention.

You will find that a little practice will enable you to review the events of the day, in a very short space of time, with a surprising degree of accuracy of detail. It seems that the mind will readily respond to this demand upon it. The process appears to be akin to a mental digestion, or rather a mental rumination, similar to that of the cow when it "chews the cud" that it has previously gathered. The thing is largely a "knack" easily acquired by a little practice. It will pay you for the little trouble and time that you expend upon it. Not only do you gain the advantage of storing away these records of the day for future use, but you also have your attention called to many important details that have escaped you, and you will find that many ideas of importance will come to you in your moments of leisure "rumination."

Let this work be done in the evening, when you feel at ease—but do not do it after you retire. The bed is made for sleep, not for thinking. You will find that the subconsciousness will awaken to the fact that it will be called upon later for the records of the day, and will, accordingly, "take notice" of what happens, in a far more diligent and faithful manner. The subconsciousness responds to a call made upon it in an astonishing manner, when it once understands just what is required of it. You will see that much of the virtue of the plan recommended consists in the fact that in the review there is an employment of the attention in a manner impossible during the haste and rush of the day's work. The faint impressions are brought out for examination, and the attention of the examination and review greatly deepen the impression in each case, so that it may be reproduced there-after. In a sentence: it is *the deepening of the faint impressions of the day.*

Thurlow Weed, a well-known politician of the nineteenth century, testifies to the efficacy of the above mentioned method, in his "Memoirs." His plan was slightly different from that mentioned by us, but you will at once see that it involves the same principles—the same psychology. Mr. Weed says: "Some of my friends used to think that I was 'cut out' for a politician, but I saw at once a fatal weakness. My memory was a sieve. I could remember nothing. Dates, names, appointments, faces—everything escaped me. I said to my wife, 'Catherine, I shall never make a successful poli-tician, for I cannot remember, and that is a prime necessity of politicians. A politician who sees a man once should remember him forever. My wife told me that I must train my memory. So when I came home that night I sat down alone and spent fifteen minutes trying silently to recall with accuracy the principal events of the day. I could remem-ber but little at first—I could not then recall what I had for breakfast. After a few days' practice I found I could recall more. Events came back to me more minutely, more accu-rately, and more vividly than at first. After a fortnight or so of this, Catherine said 'why don't you relate to me the events of the day instead of recalling them to yourself? It would be interesting and my interest in it would be a stimulus to you.' Having great respect for my wife's opinion, I began a habit of oral confession, as it were, which was continued for almost fifty years. Every night, the last thing before retiring, I told her everything I could remember that had happened to me, or about me, during the day. I generally recalled the very dishes I had for breakfast, dinner and tea; the people I had seen, and what they had said; the editorials I had written for my paper, giving her a brief abstract of them; I mentioned all the letters I had seen and received, and the very language used, as nearly as possible; when I had walked or ridden—I told her everything that had come within my observation. I found that I could say my lessons better and better every year, and instead of the practice growing irksome, it became a pleasure to go over again the events of the day. I am indebted to this discipline for a memory of unusual tenacity, and I recommend the practice to all who wish to store up facts, or expect to have much to do with influencing others."

Note that Thurlow Weed has not only given a method of recalling the particular class of occurrences mentioned in this lesson, but has also pointed out a way whereby the entire field of memory may be trained and developed. The habit of reviewing and "telling" the things that one perceives, does and thinks during the day naturally sharpens the powers of future observation, attention and perception. If you are witnessing a thing that you know that you will be called upon to describe to another person, you will instinctively apply your attention to it. The knowledge that you will be called upon for a description of a thing will give the zest of interest or necessity to it, which may be lacking otherwise. If you will "sense" things with the knowledge that you will be called upon to tell of them later on, you will give the interest and attention that go to make sharp, clear and deep impressions on the memory. In this case the seeing and hearing has "a meaning" to you, and a purpose. In addition to this, the work of review establishes a desirable habit of mind. If you don't care to relate the occurrences to another person—learn to tell them to yourself in the evening. Play the part yourself. There is a valuable secret of memory imbedded in this chapter—if you are wise enough to apply it.

Some people find it useful to keep a journal in which they write down their daily activities. What they are doing, of course, is reviewing their day in the same manner as Mr. Weed, but augmenting it by the process of writing it in their journal.

Key Points

If, every evening, you will review mentally all of give to the occurrences of each day a mental review in the evening, you will find that the act of reviewing will employ the attention to such an extent as to register the happenings in such a manner that they will be available if ever needed thereafter.

The habit of reviewing and "telling" the things that one perceives, does and thinks during the day, naturally sharpens the powers of future observation, attention and perception.

You may find it useful to keep a journal and write down your daily activities. This will provide an added tool to develop your memory.

CHAPTER 17
HOW TO REMEMBER FACTS

In speaking of this phase of memory the word "fact" is used in the sense of "an ascertained item of knowledge," rather than in the sense of "a happening," etc. In this sense the memory of facts is the ability to store away and recollect items of knowledge bearing upon some particular thing under consideration. If we are considering the subject of "horse," the "facts" that we wish to remember are the various items of information and knowledge regarding the horse, that we have acquired during our experience—facts that we have seen, heard or read, regarding the animal in question and to that which concerns it. We are continually acquiring items of information regarding all kinds of subjects, and yet when we wish to collect them we often find the task rather difficult, even though the original impressions were quite clear. The difficulty is largely due to the fact that the various facts are associated in our minds only by contiguity in time or place, or both, the associations of relation being lacking. In other words we have not properly classified and indexed our bits of information, and do not know where to begin to search for them. It is like the confusion of the business manager who kept all of his papers in a barrel, without index, or order. He knew that "they are all *there*," but he had hard work to find any one of them when it was required. Or, we are like the compositor whose type has become "pied," and then thrown into a big box—when he attempts to set up a book page, he will find it very difficult, if not impossible—whereas, if each letter were in its proper "box," he would set up the page in a short time.

This matter of association by relation is one of the most important things in the whole subject of thought, and the degree of correct and efficient thinking depends materially upon it. It does not suffice us to merely "know" a thing—we must know where to find it when we want it. An old legal adage says, "It is not so much to know the law, as to know *where to find it*." We have but little control over the associations formed by contiguity in time or space. They are in a manner accidental, depending upon the order in which the objects present themselves to the mind. On the other hand, association by similarity is largely put in our own power; for we, in a measure, select those objects that are to be associated, and bring them together in the mind. We must be careful, however, only to associate together such things as we wish to be associated together and to recall each other; and the associations we form should be based on fundamental and essential, and not upon mere superficial or casual resemblances. When things are associated by their accidental, and not by their essential qualities, by their superficial, and not by their fundamental relations, they will not be available when wanted, and will be of little real use. When we associate what is new with what most nearly resembles it in the mind already, we give it its proper place in our fabric of thought. By means of association by similarity, we tie up our ideas, as it were, in separate bundles, and it is of the utmost importance that all the ideas that most nearly resemble each other be in one bundle."

The best way to acquire correct associations, and many of them, for a separate fact that you wish to store away so that it may be recollected when needed—some useful bit of information or interesting bit of knowledge, that "may come in handy" later on—is to *analyze* it and its relations. This may be done by asking yourself questions about it—each thing that you associate it with in your answers being just one additional "cross-index" whereby you may find it readily when you want it. The principle of asking questions and obtaining answers to them may be said to characterize all intellectual effort. This is the method by which Socrates and Plato drew out the knowledge of their pupils, filling in the gaps and attaching new facts to those already known. When you wish to so consider a fact, ask yourself the following questions about it:

Where did it come from or originate,
What caused it?
What history or record does it have?
What are its attributes, qualities and characteristics?
What things can I most readily associate with it?
What is it like?

What is it good for—how may it be used—what can I do with it?
What does it prove—what can be deduced from it?
What are its natural results—what happens because of it?
What is its future and its natural or probable end or finish?
What do I think of it, on the whole—what are my general
    impressions regarding it?
What do I know about it, in the way of general information?
What have I heard about it, and from whom, and when?

If you will take the trouble to put any "fact" through the above rigid examination, you will not only attach it to hundreds of convenient and familiar other facts, so that you will remember it readily upon occasion, but you will also create a new subject of general information in your mind of which this particular fact will be the central thought.

The more other facts that you manage to associate with any one fact, the more pegs will you have to hang your facts upon—the more "loose ends" will you have whereby to pull that fact into the field of consciousness—the more cross indexes will you have whereby you may "run down" the fact when you need it. The more associations you attach to a fact, the more "meaning" does that fact have for you, and the more interest will be created regarding it in your mind. Moreover, by so doing, you make very probable the "automatic" or involuntary recollection of that fact when you are thinking of some of its associated subjects; that is, it will come into your mind naturally in connection with something else—in a "that reminds me" fashion. And the oftener that you are involuntarily "reminded" of it, the clearer and deeper its impression becomes on the records of your memory. The oftener you use a fact, the easier does it become to recall it when needed. And the more associations that you bestow upon a fact, the oftener is it likely to be used.

Another point to be remembered is that the future association of a fact depends very much upon your system of filing away facts. If you will *think* of this when endeavoring to store away a fact for future reference, you will be very apt to find the best mental pigeonhole for it. File it away with *the thing it most resembles,* or to which it has the most familiar relationship. The child does this, involuntarily—it is nature's own way. For instance, the child sees a zebra, it files away that animal as "a donkey with stripes;" a giraffe as a "long-necked horse;" a camel as a "horse with long, crooked legs, long neck and humps on its back." The child always attaches its new knowledge or fact on to some familiar fact or bit of knowledge—sometimes the result is startling, but the child remembers by means of it nevertheless. The grown up children will do well to build similar connecting links of memory. Attach the new thing to some old familiar thing. It is easy when you once have the knack of it. The table of questions previously given will bring to mind many connecting links. Use them.

If you need any proof of the importance of association by relation, and of the laws governing its action, you have but to recall the ordinary "train of thought" or "chain of images" in the mind, of which we become conscious when we are daydreaming or indulging in reverie, or even in general thought regarding any subject.

Every mental image or idea, or recollection is associated with and connected to the preceding thought and the one following it. It is a chain that is endless, until something breaks into the subject from outside. A fact flashes into your mind, apparently from space and without any reference to anything else. In such cases you will find that it occurs either because you had previously set your subconscious mentality at work upon some problem, or bit of recollection, and the flash was the belated and delayed result; or else that the fact came into your mind because of its association with some other fact, which in turn came from a precedent one, and so on. You hear a distant railroad whistle and you think of a train; then of a journey; then of some distant place; then of some one in that place; then of some event in the life of that person; then of a similar event in the life of another person; then of that other person; then of his or her brother; then of that brother's last business venture; then of that business; then of some other business resembling it; then of some people in that other business; then of their dealings with a person you know; then of the fact that another person of a similar name to the last one owes you some money; then of your determination to get that money; then you make a memorandum to place the claim in the hands of a lawyer to see whether it cannot be collected now, although your debtor was "execution proof" last year—from distant locomotive whistle to the possible collection of the account. And yet, the links forgotten, you will say that you "just happened to think of the debtor, or that it somehow flashed right into your mind," etc. But it was nothing but the law of association—that's all. Moreover, you will now find that whenever you hear mentioned the term "association of mental ideas," etc., you will remember the above illustration or part of it. We have forged a new link in the chain of association for you, and years from now it will appear in your thoughts.

Key Points

The memory of facts is the ability to store away and recollect items of knowledge bearing upon some particular thing under consideration.

When we associate what is new with what most nearly resembles it in the mind already, we give it its proper place in our fabric of thought. By means of association by similarity, we tie up our ideas, as it were, in separate bundles, and it is of the utmost importance that all the ideas that most nearly resemble each other be in one bundle.

The best way to acquire correct associations for a separate fact that you wish to store away so that it may be recollected when needed or some useful bit of information or interesting bit of knowledge that "may come in handy" later on—is to *analyze* it and its relations. This may be done by asking yourself questions about it—each thing that you associate it with in your answers being just one additional "cross-index" whereby you may find it readily when you want it.

Learn as many facts about a situation as you can. The more associations that you bestow upon a fact, the oftener is it likely to be used.

Every mental image or idea, or recollection is associated with and connected to the preceding thought and the one following it. It is a chain that is endless, until something breaks into the subject from outside. A fact flashes into your mind, apparently from space and without any reference to anything else. In such cases you will find that it occurs either because you had previously set your subconscious mentality at work upon some problem, or bit of recollection, and the flash was the belated and delayed result; or else that the fact came into your mind because of its association with some other fact, which in turn came from a precedent one, and so on.

CHAPTER 18
HOW TO REMEMBER WORDS, ETC.

In a preceding chapter a number of instances were cited of persons who had highly developed their memory of words, sentences, etc. History is full of instances of this kind. The moderns fall far behind the ancients in this respect, probably because there does not exist the present necessity for the feats of memory that were once accepted as commonplace and not out of the ordinary. Among ancient people, when printing was unknown and manuscripts scarce and valuable, it was the common custom of the people to learn "by heart" the various sacred teachings of their respective religions. The sacred books of the Hindus were transmitted in this way, and it was a common thing among the Hebrews to be able to recite the books of Moses and the Prophets entirely from memory. Even to this day the faithful Muslims are taught to commit the entire Koran to memory. The process of committing these sacred books to memory, and recalling them at will was achieved by using the natural method, instead of an artificial one.

This natural method of memorizing words, sentences, or verses is not easy. It is a system that must be mastered by steady work and faithful review. You must start at the beginning and work your way up. But the result of such work will astonish anyone not familiar with it. It is the very same method that the Hindus, Hebrews, Muslims, Norsemen, and the rest of the races, memorized their thousands of verses and hundreds of chapters of the sacred books of their people. It is the method of the successful actor, and the popular elocutionist, not to mention those speakers who carefully commit to memory their "impromptu" addresses and "extemporaneous" speeches.

This natural system of memorizing is based upon the principle that has already been alluded to in this book, and by which every child learns its alphabet and its multiplication table, as well as the little "piece" that it recites for the entertainment of its fond parents and the bored friends of the family.

This principle consists of the learning of one line at a time, and reviewing that line; then learning a second line and reviewing that; and then reviewing the two lines together; and so on, each addition being reviewed in connection with those that went before. The child learns the sound of "A;" then it learns "B;" then it associates the sounds of "A, B" in its first review; the "C" is added and the review runs: "A, B, C." And so on until "Z" is reached, The child is then able to review the entire list from "A to Z," inclusive. The multipli-cation table begins with its "2 x 1 is 2, then 2 x 2 is 4," and so on, a little at a time until the "twos" are finished and the "threes" begun. This process is kept up, by constant addition and constant review, until "12 x 12" finishes up the list, and the child is able to repeat the "tables" from first to last from memory.

But there is more to it, in the case of the child, than merely learning to repeat the alphabet or the multiplication table—there is also the strengthening of the memory as a result of its exercise and use. Memory, like every faculty of the mind, or every muscle of the body, improves and devel-ops by intelligent and reasonable use and exercise. Not only does this exercise and use develop the memory along the particular line of the faculty used, but also along *every* line and faculty. This is so because the exercise develops the power of concentration, and the use of the voluntary attention.

If you wish to acquire a good memory for words, sen-tences, etc., begin at once; select some favorite poem for the purpose of the demonstration. Then memorize one verse of not over four to six lines to begin with. Learn this verse perfectly, line by line, until you are able to repeat it with-out a mistake. Be sure to be "letter perfect" in that verse—so perfect that you will "see" even the capital letters and the punctuation marks when you recite it. Then stop for the day. The next day repeat the verse learned the day before, and then memorize a second verse in the same way, and just as perfectly. Then review the first and second verses together.

This addition of the second verse to the first serves to weld the two together by association, and each review of them together serves to add a little bit to the weld, until they become joined in the *mind* as are "A, B, C." The third day, learn a third verse, in the same way and then review the three. Continue this for say a month, 'adding a new verse each day and adding it to the verses preceding it. But constantly review them from beginning to end. You cannot review them too often. You will be able to have them flow along like the letters of the alphabet, from "A" to "Z" if you review properly and often enough.

Then, begin the second month by learning *two verses* each day, and adding to those that precede them, with constant and faithful reviews. You will find that you can memorize two verses, in the second month, as easily as you did the one verse in the first month. Your memory has been trained to this extent. And so, you may proceed from month to month, adding an extra verse to your daily task, until you are unable to spare the time for all the work, or until you feel satisfied with what has been accomplished. Use moderation and do not try to become a phenomenon. Avoid overstraining. After you have memorized the entire poem, start with a new one, but do not forget to revive the old one at frequent intervals. If you find it impossible to add the necessary number of new verses, by reason of other occupation, etc. Do not fail to keep up your review work. The exercise and review is more important than the mere addition of so many new verses.

Vary the verses, or poems with prose selections. You may start your approach to memorizing verses with a few shorter poems such as the ones presented at the end of this chapter. Then move on to longer pieces. The verses of the Bible very well adapted for such exercise, as they lend themselves easily to registration in the memory. Shakespeare's plays or The "Rubaiyat" of Omar Khayyam; or the "Lady of the Lake" by Scott, or a prose piece such as Martin Luther King's "I have a dream" speech, are well adapted to this system of memorizing.

To look at the complete poem (any of those mentioned) it would seem almost impossible that you would ever be able to memorize and recite it from beginning to end, letter perfect. But on the principle of the continual dripping of water wearing away the stone; or the snowball increasing at each roll, this practice of a little being associated to what you already have will soon allow you to accumulate a wonderfully large store of memorized verses, poems, recitations, etc.

After you have acquired quite a large assortment of memorized selections, you will find it impossible to review them all at one time. But be sure to review them all at intervals, no matter how many days may elapse between each review.

Once you have familiarized himself with the principles upon which memory depends, as given in the preceding chapters, you will see at once that the three principles of attention, association and repetition are employed in the natural method of memory improvement.

Attention must be given in order to memorize each verse in the first place; *association* is employed in the relationship created between the old verses and the new ones; and *repetition* is employed by the frequent reviewing, which serves to deepen the memory impression each time the poem is repeated.

Moreover, the principle of interest is invoked, in the gradual progress made, and the accomplishment of what at first seemed to be an impossible task—the game element is thus supplied, which serves as an incentive. These combined principles render this method an ideal one, and it is not to be wondered that it has been recognized from the earliest times.

Poems To Start Your Memorizing Regimen

The editor selected these poems because they are relatively easy to memorize and because they are inspirational, they will motivate you.

A PSALM OF LIFE

Henry Wadsworth Longfellow (1807–1882)

Tell me not, in mournful numbers,
 Life is but an empty dream! —
For the soul is dead that slumbers,
 And things are not what they seem.

Life is real! Life is earnest!
 And the grave is not its goal;
Dust thou art, to dust returnest,
 Was not spoken of the soul.

Not enjoyment, and not sorrow,
 Is our destined end or way;
But to act, that each to-morrow
 Find us farther than today.

Art is long, and Time is fleeting,
 And our hearts, though stout and brave,
Still, like muffled drums, are beating
 Funeral marches to the grave.

In the world's broad field of battle,
    In the bivouac of Life,
Be not like dumb, driven cattle!
    Be a hero in the strife!

Trust no Future, howe'er pleasant!
    Let the dead Past bury its dead!
Act, — act in the living Present!
    Heart within, and God o'erhead!

Lives of great men all remind us
    We can make our lives sublime,
And, departing, leave behind us
    Footprints on the sands of time ;

Footprints, that perhaps another,
    Sailing o'er life's solemn main,
A forlorn and shipwrecked brother,
    Seeing, shall take heart again.

Let us, then, be up and doing,
    With a heart for any fate;
Still achieving, still pursuing,
    Learn to labor and to wait.

INVICTUS

William Ernest Henley (1849–1903)

Out of the night that covers me
    Black as a pit from pole to pole
I thank whatever gods may be
    For my unconquerable soul.

In the fell clutch of circumstance
    I have not winced nor cried aloud
Under the bludgeonings of chance
    My head is bloody but unbowed

Beyond this place of wrath and tears
    Looms but the horror of the shade
And yet the menace of the years
    Finds and shall find me unafraid

It matters not how strait the gate
    How charged with punishments the scroll.
I am the master of my fate
    I am the captain of my soul.

Key Points

The natural system of memorizing is based upon the principle that consists of the learning of one line at a time, and reviewing that line; then learning a second line and reviewing that; and then reviewing the two lines together; and so on, each addition being reviewed in connection with those that went before.

If you wish to acquire a good memory for words, sentences, etc., begin at once; select some favorite poem for the purpose of the demonstration. Then memorize one verse of not over four to six lines to begin with. Learn this verse perfectly, line by line, until you are able to repeat it without a mistake.

Constantly review what you have memorized from beginning to end. You cannot review them too often. You will be able to have them flow along like the letters of the alphabet, from "A" to "Z" if you review properly and often enough.

CHAPTER 19

HOW TO REMEMBER BOOKS, PLAYS, TALES, ETC.

In the preceding chapters you learned about the development of the principal forms of memory. But there are still other phases or forms of memory, which while coming under the general classification may be still considered as worthy of special consideration. For instance there may be suggestions given regarding the memorization of the contents of the books you read, the stories you hear, etc. Let's now look at these various phases of memory.

Many of us fail to remember the important things in the books we read, and are often mortified by our ignorance regarding the contents of the works of leading authors, or of popular novels, which although we have read, we have failed to impress upon the records of our memory. The first, review the previous discussions of interest and attention. These principles of memory are basic to your endeavor.

The trouble with the majority of people is that they read books "to kill time," as a sort of mental narcotic or anesthetic, instead of for the purpose of obtaining something of interest from them. By this course we not only lose all that may be of importance or value in the book, but also acquire the habit of careless reading and inattention. The prevalence of the habit of reading many newspapers and trashy novels is responsible for the apparent inability of many persons to intelligently absorb and remember the contents of a "worth while" book when they do happen to take up such a one. But, still, even the most careless reader may cure the habit of inattention and careless reading.

We have not *read* an author till we have seen his or her object, whatever it may be, as he or she *saw* it. Read with attention. This is the rule that takes precedence of all others. It stands instead of a score of minor directions. Indeed it comprehends them all, and is the golden rule.

The page should be read as if it were never to be seen a second time; the mental eye should be fixed as, if there were no other object to think of; the memory should grasp the facts like a vise; the impressions should be distinctly and sharply received. It is not necessary, nor is it advisable to attempt to *memorize the* text of a book, excepting, perhaps, a few passages that may seem worthy to be treasured up word for word. The principal thing to be remembered about a book is it's *meaning—what* it is about. Then may follow the general outline, and the details of the story, essay, treatise or whatever it may be. The question that should be asked oneself, after the book is completed, or after the completion of some particular part of the book, is: "What was the writer's idea—what did the writer wish to say?" Get the *idea* of the writer. By taking this mental attitude you practically place yourself in the place of the writer, and thus *take part in* the idea of the book. You thus view it from the inside, rather than from the outside. You place yourself at the center of the thing, instead of upon its circumference.

If the book is a history, biography, autobiography, narrative, or story of fact or fiction, you will find it of value to visualize its occurrences as the story unfolds. That is, endeavor to form at least a faint mental picture of the events related, so that you see them "in your mind's eye," or imagination. Use your imagination in connection with the mechanical reading. In this way you build up a series of mental pictures, which will be impressed upon your mind, and which will be remembered just as are the scenes of a play that you have witnessed, or an actual event that you have seen, only less distinct of course. Particularly you should endeavor to form a clear mental picture of each character, until each one is endowed with at least a semblance of reality to you. By doing this you will impart naturalness to the events of the story and you will obtain a new pleasure from your reading. Of course, this plan will make you read more slowly, and many trashy tales will cease to interest you, for they do not contain the real elements of interest—but this is no loss, but is a decided gain for you.

At the end of each reading, take the time to mentally review the progress of the story—let the characters and scenes pass before your mental vision as in a moving picture. And when the book is finally completed, review it as a whole. By following this course, you will not only acquire the habit of easily remembering the tales and books that you have read, but will also obtain much pleasure by re-reading favorite stories in your imagination, years after. You will find that your favorite characters will take on a new reality for you, and will become as old friends in whose company you may enjoy yourself at any time, and whom you may dismiss when they tire you, without offense.

In the case of scientific treatises, essays, etc., you may follow a similar plan by dividing the work into small sections and mentally reviewing the *thought*—(not the words) of each section until you make it your own; and then by adding new sections to your review, you may gradually absorb and master the entire work. All this requires time, work and patience, but you will be repaid for your expenditure. You will find that this plan will soon render you impatient at books of little consequence, and will drive you to the best books on any given subject. You will begin to begrudge your time and attention, and hesitate about bestowing them upon any but the very best books. But in this you gain.

In order to fully acquaint yourself with a book, before reading it you should familiarize yourself with its general character. To do this you should pay attention to the full title, and the sub-title, if there be any; the name of the author and the list of other books that he or she has written, if they are noted on the title page, or the one preceding it, according to the usual custom. You should read the preface and study carefully the table of contents, that you may know the field or general subject covered by the book—in other words endeavor to get the general outline of the book, into which you may afterwards fill in the details.

In reading a book of serious import, you should make it a point to fully grasp the meaning of each paragraph before passing on to the next one. Let nothing pass you that you do not understand, at least in a general way. Consult the dictionary for words not familiar to you, so that you may grasp the full idea intended to be expressed. At the end of each chapter, section and part, you should review that which you have read, until you are able to form a mental picture of the general ideas contained therein.

To those who wish to remember the dramatic productions that they have attended, apply the principles suggested for the memory of books to this form of memory. By taking an interest in each character as it appears; by studying carefully each action and scene, and then reviewing each act in the intervals between the acts; and by finally reviewing the entire play after your return home, you will fasten the whole play as a complete mental picture, on the records of your memory. If you have acquainted yourself with what has just been said regarding the recollection of the contents of books, you will be able to modify and adapt them to the purpose of recollecting plays and dramatic productions. You will find that the oftener you review a play, the more clearly will you remember it. Many little details overlooked at first will come into the field of consciousness and fit into their proper places.

Sermons, lectures and other discourses may be remembered by bestowing interest and attention upon them, and by attempting to grasp each general idea advanced, and by noting the passage from one general idea to another. If you will practice this a few times, you will find that when you come to review the discourse (and this you should always do—it is the natural way of developing memory) the little details will come up and fit into their proper places. In this form of memory, the important thing is to train the memory by exercise and review. You will find that at each review of a discourse you will have made progress. By practice and exercise, the subconscious mentality will do better work, and will show that it is rising to its new responsibilities. You have allowed it to sleep during the many discourses to which you have listened, and it must be taught new habits. Let it know that it is expected to retain that which it hears, and then exercise it frequently by reviews of discourses, and you will be surprised at the degree of the work it will perform for you. Not only will you remember better, but also you will *hear* better and more intelligently. The subconsciousness, knowing that it will be called upon later on to recollect what is being said, will urge you to bestow the attention necessary to supply it with the proper material.

To those who have had trouble in remembering discourses, we urge that they should begin to attend lectures and other forms of discourse, with the distinct purpose of developing that form of memory. Give to the sub-conscious mentality the positive command that it shall attend to what is being said, and shall record the same in such a way that when you review the discourse afterward you will be presented with a good synopsis or syllabus of it. You should avoid any attempt to memorize the *words* of the discourse—your purpose being to absorb and record the *ideas* and general thought expressed. Interest—Attention—Practice—Review—these are the important points in memory.

To remember stories, anecdotes, fables, etc., apply the principles given above. The main thing in memorizing an anecdote is to be able to catch the *fundamental idea* underlying it, and the epigrammatic sentence, or central phrase, which forms the "point" of the story. Be sure that you catch these perfectly, and then commit the "point" to memory. If necessary make a memorandum of the point, until you have opportunity to review the story in your mind. Then carefully review it mentally, repeating it to yourself in your own words. By rehearsing and reviewing the story, you make it your own and will be able to relate it afterward just as you would something that you had actually experienced. So true is this principle, that when carried too far it endows the story with a false sense of actuality. Do not carry the principle to this extreme but use it in moderation. The trouble with many people is that they attempt to repeat a tale, long after they have heard it, without reviewing or rehearsing in the meantime. Consequently they omit many important points, because they have failed to impress the story as a whole upon the memory. In order to *know* an anecdote properly, you should be able to *see* its characters and incidents, just as you do when you see an illustrated joke in a comic paper. If you can make a mental picture of an anecdote, you will be apt to remember it with ease. Really good story tellers review and rehearse their jokes, and have been known to try them on their unsuspecting friends in order to get the benefit of practice before relating them in public. It saves one the mortification of being compelled to finish up a long-drawn out tale by an "Er—well, um-m-m—I'm afraid I've forgotten just how that story ended—but it was a good one!"

Key Points

Read with attention. This is the rule that takes precedence of all others. It stands instead of a score of minor directions. Indeed it comprehends them all, and is the golden rule.

It is not necessary, nor is it advisable to attempt to *memorize the* text of a book, excepting, perhaps, a few passages that may seem worthy to be treasured up word for word. The principal thing to be remembered about a book is its *meaning—what* it is about

If the book is a history, biography, autobiography, narrative, or story of fact or fiction, you will find it of value to visualize it's occurrences as the story unfolds.

In order to fully acquaint yourself with a book, before reading it you should familiarize yourself with its general character. To do this you should pay attention to the full title, and the sub-title, if there be any. You should read the preface and study carefully the table of contents.

When listening to a sermon, speech or discourse, attend to what is said, and record it in your mind so that when you review it afterwards, you will be presented with a good synopsis of it. Your objective is to absorb and record the *ideas* and general thought expressed. Interest—Attention—Practice—Review— these are the important points in memory.

CHAPTER 20

GENERAL INSTRUCTIONS

This chapter may be considered in the nature of a general review of certain fundamental principles mentioned in the body of the work.

POINT 1. *Give to the thing that you wish to memorize, as great a degree of concentrated attention as possible.*

The degree of concentrated attention bestowed upon the object under consideration, determines the strength, clearness and depth of the impression received and stored away in the subconsciousness. The character of these stored away impressions determines the degree of ease in remembrance and recollection.

POINT 2. *In considering an object to be memorized, endeavor to obtain the impressions through as many faculties and senses as possible.*

An impression received through both sound and sight is doubly as strong as one received through only one of these channels. You may remember a name, or word, either by having seen it in writing or print; or else by reason of having heard it; but if you have both *seen and heard it* you have a double impression, and possess two possible ways of reviving the impression. You are able to remember an orange by reason of having seen it, smelt it, felt it and tasted it, and having heard its name pronounced. Endeavor to know a thing from as many sense impressions as possible—use the eye to assist ear impressions; and the ear to assist in eye impressions. See the thing from as many angles as possible.

POINT 3. *Exercising the particular faculty through which the weak impressions are received may strengthen sense impressions.*

You will find that either your eye memory is better than your ear memory, or vice versa. The remedy lies in exercising the weaker faculty, so as to bring it up to the standard of the stronger. The chapters of eye and ear training will help you along these lines. The same rule applies to the several phases of memory—develop the weak ones, and the strong ones will take care of themselves. The only way to develop a sense or faculty is to intelligently train, exercise and use it. Use, exercise and practice will work miracles in this direction.

POINT 4. *Make your first impression strong and firm enough to serve as a basis for subsequent ones.*

Get into the habit of *fixing* a clear, strong impression of a thing to be considered, from the first. Otherwise you are trying to build up a large structure upon a poor foundation. Each time you revive an impression you deepen it, but if you have only a dim impression to begin with, the deepened impression will not include details omitted in the first one. It is like taking a good sharp negative of a picture that you intend to enlarge afterward. The details lacking in the small picture will not appear in the enlargement; but those that *do* appear in the small one, will be enlarged with the picture.

POINT 5. *Revive your impressions frequently and thus deepen them.*

You will know more of a picture by seeing it a few minutes every day for a week, than you would by spending several hours before it at one time. So it is with the memory. By recalling an impression a number of times, you fix it indelibly in your mind in such a way that it may be readily found when needed. Such impressions are like favorite tools that you need every little while—they are not apt to be mislaid, as are those that are but seldom used. Use your imagination in "going over" a thing that you wish to remember. If you are studying a thing, you will find that this "going over" in your imagination will help you materially in disclosing the things that you have not remembered about it. By thus recognizing your weak points of memory, you may be able to pick up the missing details when you study the object itself the next time.

POINT 6. *Use your memory and place confidence in it.*

One of the important things in the cultivation of the memory is the actual use of it. Begin to trust it a little, and then more, and then still more, and it will rise to the occasion. Those who have to tie a string around a finger in order to remember certain things, soon begin to cease to use their memory, and in the end forget to remember the string, or what it is for. There are many details, of course, with which it is folly to charge the memory, but you should never allow your memory to fall into disuse. If you are in an occupation in which the work is done with mechanical aid, then you should exercise the memory by learning verses, or other things, in order to keep it in active practice. Do not allow your memory to atrophy.

POINT 7. *Establish as many associations for an impression, as possible.*

Association is memory's method of indexing and cross-indexing. Each association renders it easier to remember or recollect the thing. Each association gives you another string to your mental bow. Endeavor to associate a new bit of knowledge with something already known by, and familiar to you. In this way to avoid the danger of having the thing isolated and alone in your mind—without a label, or index number and name, connect your object or thought to be remembered with other objects or thoughts, by the association of contiguity in space and time, and by relationship of kind, resemblance or oppositeness. You will often be able to remember a thing by remembering something else that happened at the same place, or about the same time—these things give you the "loose ends" of rec-ollection whereby you may unwind the ball of memory. In the same way, one is often able to recollect names by slowly running over the alphabet, with a pencil, until the sight of the capital first letter of the name brings the mem-ory of those following it—this, however, only when the name has previously been memorized by sight. In the same way the first few notes of a musical selection will enable you to remember the whole air; or the first words of a sen-tence, the entire speech or selection following it. In trying to remember a thing that has escaped you, you will find it helpful to think of something associated with that thing, even remotely. A little practice will enable you to recollect the thing along the lines of the faintest association or clue. Some people are adept memory detectives, following this plan. The "loose end" in memory is all the expert requires. Any associations furnish these loose ends. An interest-ing and important fact to remember in this connection is that if you have some one thing that tends to escape your memory, you may counteract the trouble by noting the associated things that have previously served to bring it into mind with you. The associated thing once noted, may thereafter be used as a loose end with which to unwind the elusive fact or impression. This idea of association is quite fascinating when you begin to employ it in your memory exercises and work. And you will find many little methods of using it. But always use natural association, and avoid the temptation of endeavoring to tie your memory up with the red tape of the artificial systems.

POINT 8. *Group your impressions.*

This is but a form of association, but is very important. If you can arrange your bits of knowledge and fact into logical groups, you will always be master of your subject. By associating your knowledge with other knowledge along the same general lines, both by resemblances and by opposites, you will be able to find what you need just when you need it. Napoleon Bonaparte had a mind trained along these lines. He said that his memory was like a large case of small drawers and pigeonholes, in which he filed his information according to its kind. In order to do this he used the methods mentioned in this book of comparing the new thing with the old ones, and then deciding into which group it naturally fitted. This is largely a matter of practice and knack, but it may be acquired by a little thought and care, aided by practice. And it will repay one well for the trouble in acquiring it. The following table will be found useful in classifying objects, ideas, facts, etc., so as to correlate and associate them with other facts of a like kind. The table is to be used in the line of questions addressed to oneself regarding the thing under consideration. It somewhat resembles the table of questions given in Chapter 17 of this book, but has the advantage of brevity. Memorize this table and use it.

QUERY TABLE.

Ask yourself the following questions regarding the thing under consideration. It will draw out many bits of information and associated knowledge in your mind:

WHAT?

WHEN?

WHERE?

WHEN?

HOW?

WHY?

While the above six queries are given you as a means of acquiring clear impressions and associations, they will also serve as a Magic Key to Knowledge, if you use them intelligently. If you can answer these questions regarding anything, you will know a great deal about that particular thing. And after you have answered them fully, there will be but little unexpressed knowledge regarding that thing left in your memory.

BOOK II

Practical Mental Influence

Mental Vibrations, Psychic Influence,
Personal Magnetism, Fascination,
Psychic Self-Protection, etc.

CONTENTS

PREFACE

We have within us the power to influence others by projecting our thoughts to them and contrariwise others can attempt to influence us in the same manner. This is not magic or fantasy. Thoughts flow from one person to another just as audio and video waves flow through the atmosphere. In ancient times, this phenomenon appeared to be "white magic." If used for good purposes, or "black magic" or witchcraft, if used for evil. Today we know that this is scientifically possible.

Radio, television, cell phones and other modern inventions have proven that electrical waves travel through space. Science has also shown that this is true of thought-waves.

All students of mental influence have noticed the close resemblance that is manifested between the phenomena of electrical and magnetic energy on the one hand and the phenomenon of mental energy on the other. Investigators of mental influence have demonstrated by their experiments that there is such a thing as thought-induction, and many other phases of manifestation similar to that exhibited by electricity and magnetism.

The mind, in its manifestation of thought in the brain, generates a form of energy of intensely high vibration, which energy is projected in vibratory waves from the brains of other persons within its field of influence.

This transference of thought from one person to another is not limited to close contact between people. It is a scientific fact that people can transmit an idea to another brain from a distance.

In this book you will learn how you can dominate others with your thoughts and protect yourself from undue influence of people who wish to dominate you.

CHAPTER 1

THE LAW OF VIBRATION

Students of history find a continuous chain of reference to the mysterious influence of one human mind over that of others. In the earliest records, traditions and legends may be found giving reference to the general belief that it was possible for an individual to exert some weird uncanny power over the minds of other persons, which would influence the latter for good or evil. And more than this, the student will find an accompanying belief that certain individuals are possessed of some mental power which bends even "things" and circumstances to its might.

Way back in the dim past of human history on this planet, this belief existed, and it has steadily persisted in spite of the strenuous opposition of material science, even unto the present day. The years have not affected the belief, and in these dawning days of the twenty-first century it has taken on a new strength and vitality, for its adherents have boldly stepped to the front, and confronting the doubting materialistic thinkers, have claimed the name of "Science" for this truth and have insisted that it be taken, once and for all, from the category of superstition, credulity and ignorant phantasm.

Were it not pitiable, it would be amusing to glance at the presumptuous, complacent, smug, self-satisfied position of the materialistic school of thinkers, who brush aside as a foolish delusion that which many of the wisest scholars of a past age have accepted and taught as the truth. The modern "know-it-alls" sneer contemptuously at facts that are known to be of actual occurrence in the daily lives of thousands of intelligent people, and which the experience of humankind has demonstrated for many centuries, in all lands and all races.

The trouble lies in the dogmatic assumption of the materialistic school that what is known as "mind" is merely some peculiar action of the material brain, some writers even holding that "the brain secretes thought, just as the liver secretes bile." They refuse to see that the operation of *mind* is a manifestation of energy known as electricity, magnetism, light, heat, gravitation, cohesion, etc. Because mental energy does not register the vibrations of these lower forms of energy, they conclude that the higher mental energy does not exist. Having formulated a theory to suit their materialistic conceptions, they try to ignore all facts not consistent with their theory. If they find a fact that will not squeeze into their narrow theory they promptly ignore or dispute it.

As a matter of truth, the investigator is not compelled to resort to metaphysical explanations to account for the phenomena of mental influence. The very facts of physical science itself, if rightly interpreted, will give the clue to the mystery; and will point the steps of the honest investigator toward the solution of the perplexing riddle. Although we know that the real solution lies in the metaphysical realm, still even physical science will corroborate the facts of its metaphysical sister science, and instead of contradicting the latter will actually go far toward furnishing analogous facts and principles basis for a theory of metaphysical facts.

The student will see at once that so far as physical science is concerned, it must begin at the phenomenon of *thought transference*, for in that phase of the subject may be found an elementary principle in evidence in many other forms of phenomena.. The main fact is that thought transference does exist, and may be accounted for upon purely scientific grounds, without calling in the truths of metaphysical thought. In the first place, physical science teaches that underlying all forms, degrees and apparent differences in matter and energy, there is to be found a manifestation of some elementary energy, which manifests in what is known as *vibrations*. Everything in the material world is in vibration— ever manifesting a high degree of motion. Without vibration there would be no such thing as a material universe. From the electronic corpuscles which science teaches compose the atom; up through the atom and molecule, until the most complex forms of matter are manifested, there is the ever-present vibration. And through all forms of energy, light, heat, electricity, magnetism and the rest, vibration is also ever present. In fact, physical science itself teaches that not only is vibration the basic force underlying other forces and the various forms of matter, but also that the apparent differences between the various forms of matter, and also between the various forms of energy, are caused simply and solely by the varying degrees of vibration manifested.

Just as the difference between the lowest tone that can be distinguished by the human ear, and the highest note that can be distinguished by the same organ of sense, is merely a difference between the rate of vibration—just as is the difference between the dull red color at one end of the spectrum, and the violet at the other end, with the intervening colors known as indigo, blue green, yellow and orange, with all the combinations of shades arising from them—just as the difference between the greatest degree of cold known to science, and the greatest degree of heat that can be conceived of—just as these great differences due solely and wholly to varying rates of vibration—so is the difference between and all forms of matter or force simply a matter of the rate of vibration. In short, all material and physical "things" are simply manifestations of some "infinite and eternal energy from which all things proceed," their differences resulting merely from the different degree of vibration being manifested in them. Remember, that this is not "vague philosophy" or "airy metaphysics" or "spiritualistic vagaries" (to quote from the materialistic writers), but facts claimed and admitted by the greatest physical scientists of the age, as a reference to their lectures and textbooks will prove to anyone.

And, more than this, any intelligent physical scientist will tell you that Science has every reason to believe that there are great fields of energy and force, the vibrations of which are far too high for even the delicate instruments of science to record, but which nevertheless exist and manifest effects. It was only the other day that science was able to "catch" the "X-rays" and other forms of high radioactivity, and yet these rays and forces had always existed. And tomorrow science will perfect instruments capable of registering still higher forms of energy. And bye-and-bye, some scientist will perfect an instrument capable of registering and recording the subtle vibrations of thought, and perhaps in time someone will perfect that instrument so that it will not only record such thought vibrations and waves, but, like the phonograph, it will be able to reproduce and send forth similar vibrations so that others may feel the thoughts, just as they now hear the sounds from the phonograph. Such a prediction is no more wonderful then would have been the prediction of the telephone, television, microwave transmission and sundry other discoveries and inventions two hundred years ago.

Did you ever think that there are colors that the eye cannot see, but which delicate instruments clearly register? In fact, the rays of light which sunburn the face, and which register on the photographic plate are not visible to the eye. The eye sees the lower rays, but only instruments adapted for the purpose detect the higher ones. Your eye cannot see the X-ray as it passes through the room, but the plate will catch it, and its light may make a photograph. The rays of light visible to the eyes are only the lower ones—the higher ones are far beyond the power of the eye to record, and beyond even the range of the most delicate instrument there exist rays and waves of light of such high vibratory rate as to defy even its power to record.

Did you ever know that there are sounds unheard by human ears that the microphone will catch and magnify? Scientific imagination dreams of instruments that will catch the songs of the mite-like insects, and magnify them until they can be distinguished. There are waves of electricity that may pass through your body, unperceived by you, and yet powerful enough to run light electric lights. Listen to the words of certain eminent scientists.

Prof. Elisha Gary, a celebrated scientist and teacher, has said: "There is much food for speculation in the thought that there exists sound waves that no human ear can hear, and color waves of light that no eye can see. The long, dark, soundless space between 40,000 and 400,000,000,000,000 vibrations per second, and the infinity of range beyond 700,000,000,000,000 vibrations per second, where light ceases, in the universe of motion, makes it possible to indulge in speculation."

There is no gradation between the most rapid undulations or trembling that produces our sensations of sound, and the slowest of those which give rise to our sensations of gentlest warmth. There is a huge gap between them, wide enough to include another world of motion, all lying between our world of sound and our world of heat and light; and there is no good reason whatever for supposing that matter is incapable of such intermediate activity, or that such activity may not give rise to intermediate sensations, provided that there are organs for taking up and sensitizing their movements.

And, so you see that in the scientific theory of vibrations, there may be found plenty of room for a scientific explanation of all that is claimed by adherents of the truth of *mental influence,* without getting out of the region of physical science, and without invading the plane of metaphysics. And there are many more proofs from the same source, which we may touch upon as we proceed.

There is but one truth, and it manifests on all planes—the *spiritual*; the *mental*; and the *physical*—and manifestations agree and coincide. So no mentalist need fear the test of physical science, for each plane will bear out the facts and phenomena of the ones below or above it—the three are but varying phases of one. In this book we shall hug close to the plane of physical science, because by so doing we will be able to make the subject much clearer to many than if we had attempted to express the teaching in metaphysical terms. There is no contradiction in the end. Each bit of truth must dovetail into every other bit, for all are parts of the whole.

Key Points

Underlying all forms, degrees and apparent differences in matter and energy, there is to be found a manifestation of some elementary energy, which manifests in what is known as *vibrations*. Everything in the material world is in vibration—ever manifesting a high degree of motion. Without vibration there would be no such thing as a material universe. Vibration the basic force underlying other forces and the various forms of matter, but also that the apparent differences between the various forms of matter, and also between the various forms of energy, are caused simply and solely by the varying degrees of vibration manifested.

There is but one truth, and it manifests on all planes—the *spiritual*; the *mental*; and the *physical*—and manifestations agree and coincide. So no mentalist need fear the test of physical science, for each plane will bear out the facts and phenomena of the ones below or above it—the three are but varying phases of one.

CHAPTER 2
THOUGHT WAVES

In the last chapter we have seen that vibration was to be found underlying all manifestations of energy, and all forms of matter. We also learned that there were fields of vibratory energy not filled by any known forms of energy, the inference being that inasmuch as there are no gaps in nature's processes these unknown fields must be occupied by certain forms of energy not known as yet to physical science. The teachings of the occultists of all lands and ages, as also those of modern psychology, are to the effect that the mind, in its manifestation of thought in the brain, generates a form of energy of intensely high vibration, which energy is projected in vibratory waves from the brains of other persons within its field of influence.

All students of mental influence have noticed the close resemblance that is manifested between the phenomena of electrical and magnetic energy on the one hand and the phenomena of mental energy on the other. So close is the analogy that one may take the proven facts of science relating to electrical and magnetic phenomena and confidently proceed with the certainty of finding a strikingly close correspondence in the field of mental phenomena. And the recognition of this fact is helping the workers in the mental field group together the varied phenomena that come under their notice, and to work out the theory and practice of mental influence.

In the first place, it is now a fact well known and accepted by investigators that the generation of thought and the manifestation of mental states occasions a "burning up" of brain matter, and the consequent production of a form of energy of high vibratory power. Physiologists recognize this fact, and the textbooks make reference to it. Experiments have shown that the temperature of the brain is increased in accordance with the intensity of feeling and thought, and that there is undoubtedly a generation of energy and a consumption of brain matter which bears a very close resemblance to the process of the generation of electrical energy. And this being conceded, it follows that this energy once released must be emanated or sent forth from the brain in the manner akin to the emanation of other known forms of energy, i.e., in the form of "waves" of vibratory force. Light and heat travel in this way—so do electricity and magnetism—so do the forces of radioactivity. And the investigators of mental influence have demonstrated by their experiments that there is such a thing as thought-induction, and many other phases of manifestation similar to that exhibited by electricity and magnetism.

One mind can act at a distance upon another, without the habitual medium of words, or any other visible means of communication. There is nothing unscientific, nothing romantic in admitting that an idea can influence a brain from a distance. The action of one human being upon another, from a distance, is a scientific fact, it is as certain as the existence of Paris, of Napoleon, of oxygen, or of Sirius. There can be no doubt that our physical force creates a movement in the atmosphere which transmits itself afar like all movements in the atmosphere, becomes perceptible to brains in harmony with our own. The transformation of a psychic action into an ethereal movement, and the reverse, may be analogous to what takes place on a telephone, where the receptive plate, which is identical with the plate at the other end, reconstructs the sonorous movement transmitted, not by means of sound, but by electricity, When a thought or feeling is generated in the mind or brain of a person, the energy generated flows forth from the brain of the person in the form of waves of mental energy, spreading from the immediate neighborhood of the thinker to a distance proportioned to the strength of the thought or feeling. These thought-waves have the property of awakening similar vibrations in the minds of other persons coming within their field of force, according to the laws of mental influence. Thought-waves are manifested in a variety of forms and phases. Some are the waves emanated from the minds of all thinkers, unconsciously and without purpose, and usually without much force. Others are sent forth with great force, and travel far, manifesting a degree of influence commensurate with the force with which they are projected. Others are directed purposely toward certain individuals or places, and travel along rapidly in a straight line to the point that they have been directed or aimed. Others are sent forth with great strength and power, but instead of being directed toward any particular person or place, are designed to sweep around in great whirlpools of energy affecting all who happen to fall within their field force.

You will readily understand that there is a great difference between thought-waves sent forth idly and unconsciously, and without knowledge of the underlying laws of mental influence, and those projected with a full knowledge of the laws governing the phenomena and urged on and directed by a powerful will of the sender. The force is the same, but the degree of its power, and the measure of its effects are determined by the conditions of its sending force.

The vibratory force of these thought-waves does not cease with the sending forth of the wave, but persists for a long time afterward. Just as heat in a room persists long after the fire in the stove has been extinguished—just as the perfume of the flower exists in a room long after the flower has been removed—just as a ray of light travels through space for millions of miles, and for centuries after the star itself has been blotted out of existence—just as any and all forms of vibratory energy persist in manifesting after the initial impulse has been withdrawn—so do the vibrations of thought continue long after the thought, long after the brain which sent them forth has passed into dust.

There are many places today filled with the thought-vibrations of minds long since passed outside of the body. There are many places filled with the strong vibrations of tragedies long since enacted there. Every place has an atmosphere of its own, arising from the thought vibrations set in motion by the various persons who have inhabited or occupied them. Every city has its own mental atmosphere, which has an effect upon persons moving into them. Some are lively, some dull, some progressive, some old-fogeyish, some moral, some immoral—the result of the character of the early settlers and leading spirits of the places. The atmosphere affects persons moving into these towns, and either sinks to the general level, or else, if strong enough, help to change the mental tone of the place. Sometimes a change in conditions brings a large influx of new people to the town, and the mental waves of the newcomers tend to bring about a marked change in the local mental atmosphere. These facts have been noted by many observing people who were, perhaps, not familiar with the laws and principles underlying the phenomena.

Many have of course noticed the differing atmosphere of stores, offices and other places of business. Some of such places give one an air of confidence and trust; others create a feeling of suspicion and mistrust; some convey an impression of active, wide awake management, while others impress one as being behind the times and suffering from lack of alert, active management. Did you ever stop to think that these different atmospheres were caused by the prevailing mental attitudes of those in charge of the places? The managers of business places send forth Thought-Waves of their own, and their employees naturally falling into the pace set for them, sending forth similar vibrations, and before long the whole place is vibrating on a certain scale. Let a change in the management occur and see what a change soon manifests itself.

Did you ever notice the mental atmospheres of the houses you happened to visit? You may experience and recognize all of the varying notes in the mental scale of their occupants. From some thresholds harmony manifests itself, while others breathe in harmony as soon as you step over the threshold. Some radiate mental warmth, while others seem as cold as an iceberg. Think for a moment and recall the various houses or places you visit, and see how the mental vibrations of the inmates manifest themselves to a visitor.

The low quarters of our cities, the dens of vice and haunts of dissipation vibrate with the character of thought and feeling of those inhabiting them. And the weak-willed visitor is thus tempted. And, in the same way, certain places are filled with strong, helpful, elevating vibrations, which tend to lift up and elevate those coming within their circle of influence. Thoughts and feelings are contagious, by reason of *the law of vibration and mental induction*. When this law is understood the individual is enabled to protect and improve himself. Such knowledge brings strength.

Key Points

The mind, in its manifestation of thought in the brain, generates a form of energy of intensely high vibration, which energy is projected in vibratory waves from the brains of other persons within its field of influence, whether that person is nearby or at a distance.

When a thought or feeling is generated in the mind or brain of a person, the energy generated flows forth from the brain of the person in the form of waves of mental energy, spreading from the immediate neighborhood of the thinker to a distance proportioned to the strength of the thought or feeling. These thought-waves have the property of awakening similar vibrations in the minds of other persons coming within their field of force, according to the laws of mental influence.

Thought-waves are manifested in a variety of forms and phases. Some are the waves emanated from the minds of all thinkers, unconsciously and without purpose, and usually without much force. Others are sent forth with great force, and travel far, manifesting a degree of influence commensurate with the force with which they are projected. Others are directed purposely toward certain individuals or places, and travel along rapidly in a straight line to the point that they have been directed or aimed. Others are sent forth with great strength and power, but instead of being directed toward any particular person or place, are designed to sweep around in great whirlpools of energy affecting all who happen to fall within their field force.

CHAPTER 3
MENTAL INDUCTION

As stated in the preceding chapter, the phenomena of mental influence bears a striking analogy to that of the electrical or magnetic energy. Not only is this so in the phase of wave motion and transmission, but also in the phase of induction.

In physical science the term *induction* is used to indicate that quality in a manifestation of energy that tends to reproduce in a second object the vibrations manifesting in the first object, without direct contact between the two bodies. A magnet will induce magnetism in another object removed from its space. An electrified object will tend to produce similar vibrations in another object by induction, over great spaces. Heat waves travel along the atmosphere, and tend to produce heat vibrations in objects far removed, notably in the case of the sun and the earth. Even sound waves will affect other objects in this way, as in the well-known instance of the glass or vase "singing" in response to the musical note sounded afar off. In fact, we see and hear by processes similar to those described.

And in this same manner that thought-waves carry the vibrations of the mind sending them forth to great distances, or lesser ones, tending to set up similar vibrations in the middle of other persons within their field force. Thus a person feeling a strong degree of anger will pour forth waves of that degree of mental vibration, which, coming in contact with the brains of other persons, tend to set up a similar feelings or emotions and thus cause the person to "feel cross" or "peevish" or even to manifest a similar angry state of mind. We all know how easily a fight is started by a very angry person in a room sending forth violent vibrations. One has but to remember the instances of mob violence to see how easily the contagion of hate and anger spread among people who allow themselves to be influenced. And not only is this true of undesirable emotions and feelings, but also of desirable ones. The influence of a good man or woman who happens to be strong mentally spreads among other people, influencing in them for good.

Orators, actors, preachers and teachers emit strong currents, which tend to produce mental conditions on the part of their hearers corresponding to the feeling held by the mind of the speaker. When you remember how this speaker swayed your feelings, or how that actor made you weep with pity, shiver with fear, or laugh with joy, you will see how mental induction acts.

But not only is this true when we are in the actual presence of the person sending out the thought-waves, but it is equally true that we are influenced by persons far removed from us in space, often without their knowledge or intent, although sometimes (in the case of one who understands the principal most) with full knowledge and intent.

The atmosphere with which space is filled carries these thought-waves in all directions, and the surface of the earth, particularly in the densely occupied portions, is filled with these waves. These waves, carrying the mental vibrations, coming in contact with each other, tend to set up combinations on one hand, or else neutralize each other on the other hand. That is to say, if two sets of waves of a similar nature meet there is likely to be a combination formed between them just as between two chemicals having an affinity for each other. In this way the "mental atmosphere" of places, towns, houses, etc., is formed. On the other hand if currents of opposing vibrations came in contact with each other, there will be manifested a conflict between the two, in which each will lose in proportion to its weakness, and the result will be either a neutralization of both or else a combination having vibrations of an average rate. For instance, if two currents of mental energy meet, one being a thought of love and the other hate, they will neutralize each other if they are equal, or if one is stronger than the other, it will persist but robbed of much of its strength. If it were not for this neutralizing effect we would be largely at the mercy of stray currents of thought. Nature protects us in this way, and also by rendering us immune to a considerable extent.

But nevertheless we are affected by these waves to a considerable extent, unless we have learned to throw them off by knowledge of the laws and an enforcement of them by practice. We all know how great waves of feeling spread over the town, city or country, sweeping people off their balance. Great waves of political enthusiasm, or war spirits, or prejudice for or against certain people, or groups of people, sweep over places and cause people to act in a manner that they will afterward regret when they come to themselves and consider their acts in cold blood. Demagogues will sway them or magnetic leaders who wish to gain their votes or patronage; and they will be led into acts of mob violence, or similar atrocities, by yielding to these waves of "contagious" thought. On the other hand we all know how great waves of religious feeling sweep over a community upon the occasion of some great "revival" excitement or fervor.

The effect of these thought-waves, so far as the power of induction is concerned, of course depends very materially upon the strength of the thought or feeling being manifested in the mind sending them forth. The majority of persons put but little force into the mental manifestations, but here and there is to be found a thinker whose thought-waves are practically "a stream of living will" and which of course have a very strong inductive effect upon the minds of others with whom the waves come in contact. But it likewise follows that a number of persons thinking along the same lines will produce a great volume of power by a combination of their thought currents into great streams of mental force.

Then again there is another feature of the case that we must not lose sight of, and that is the *attraction* between minds, by virtue of which people are drawn to the thought-waves of others whose thoughts are in accord with their own. The contrary is true, for there is *repulsion* between the minds of persons and the thought-waves of others whose thoughts are not in accord with their own.

To quote a well-worn and much-used expression to illustrate this truth, "Like attracts like," and "Birds of a feather flock together." There is ever in operation this marvelous law of attraction and repulsion of mental energy. Persons allowing their thoughts to run along certain lines, and permitting the feelings to be expressed in certain ways, draw to themselves the thought-waves and mental influences of others keyed to the same mental key-note. And likewise they repel the waves and influences of an opposing nature. This is an important fact to remember in one's everyday life. Good attracts good and repels evil. Evil attracts evil and repels good. The predominant mental attitude serves to attract similar influences and to repel the opposing ones. Therefore watch carefully the character and nature of your thoughts—cultivate the desirable ones and repress the undesirable ones. As the Biblical book of Proverbs states: "As a man thinketh in his heart, so is he."

Some thought-waves sent forth with but little strength travel slowly and do not proceed very far from their place of emanation, but creep along like some smoke or fog, lazily and yielding. Other thoughts charged with a greater intensity of desire or will, dart forth vigorously like an electric spark, and often travel great distances. The weak thought-waves do not last a very long time, but fade away or become neutralized or dissipated by stronger, forces. But the strong thoughts persist for a long time, retaining much of their vitality and energy.

In the same manner our own thought-waves will continue to vibrate around us wherever we go, and those coming in contact with us will be impressed by the character of our vibrations in this way. Some people send forth gloomy vibrations in this way, which you feel when you come in contact with them. Others radiate good-cheer, courage and happiness, which conditions are induced in those with whom they come in contact. Many people will manifest these qualities so strongly that one can notice the effect the moment such persons enter a room. They carry their atmosphere with them, and the same is induced in the minds of others around them.

In the same way some people carry with them vibrations of will power and strength that beat upon the minds of others. This makes them feel the power of such persons and it conquers their own will power and changes their desires. Others manifest a strong power of fascination or attraction, in a similar manner that tends to draw others to them and to their desires and wishes. Not only does this principle operate in the phase of general mental atmospheres, but also in the phase of direct personal influence.

All forms of mental influence operate along the lines of mental induction. The principle is the same in all cases and instances, although the manner of operation varies according to the particular phase of the phenomena manifested. Remember this as we proceed, and you will be able to understand the subject much better.

Key Points

Thought-waves carry the vibrations of the mind sending them forth to great distances, or lesser ones, tending to set up similar vibrations in the middle of other persons within their field force.

Not only is this true when we are in the actual presence of the person sending out the thought-waves, but it is equally true that we are influenced by persons far removed from us in space, often without their knowledge or intent.

Some people send forth gloomy vibrations in this way, which you feel when you come in contact with them. Others radiate good-cheer, courage and happiness, which conditions are induced in those with whom they come in contact.

CHAPTER 4

MENTAL CONCENTRATION

The two principal factors in the manifestation of mental influence, in all of its forms, are what are know as (1) *Concentration*, and (2) *Mental Imagining*. The first of these factors shall be considered in this chapter, the succeeding chapter taking up the consideration of the second.

"Concentration" is a word derived from two Latin words: "con," a prefix meaning "to;" and "centrum," meaning "center" or "fixed central point." The two words combined mean, literally, "to bring to a common point; to focus," etc. Thus the word "concentration" is seen to mean, literally, "the act or state of bringing to a fixed point or focus.

Borrowing an analogous illustration from physical science, we readily see that the highest forms of energy, force or power are manifested by bringing the force to a focus, center, or common point thereby directing to that point the entire energy employed, instead of allowing it to become dissipated over a larger area. The electricity generated by a battery or dynamo, if allowed to diffuse itself over a large surface manifests but a small degree of the power that may be obtained from it by compelling it to discharge itself from a small point of focus. The same is true regarding the power of steam, which manifests great power by being forced to discharge itself through a small point or opening instead of being permitted to spread itself widely in the air. The same law applies to gunpowder, which manifests force by its gases being compelled to escape through the small gun-barrel instead of spreading in all directions, which it would do if unconfined. Another familiar example is that of the sun-glass, or "burning-glass," which brings the rays of the sun to a common point or focus, greatly intensifying the heat and light by reason thereof.

The occult masters have ever impressed upon their pupils the importance and necessity of acquiring the power of mental concentration, and all trained and developed occultists have practiced and persevered toward this end, the result being that some of them attained almost miraculous mental powers and influence. All occult phenomena are caused in this way, and all occult power depends upon it. Therefore the student of mental influence should devote much thought, time and practice to this most important branch of the subject.

It is a fact known to all students of mental phenomena that very few persons possess more than a very small degree of concentration. They allow their mental forces to become scattered and dissipated in all directions, and obtain little or no results from the same. In the degree that we are able to concentrate, so are we able to manifests mental power. Our power of mental concentration is to a great extent our measure of greatness.

Mental concentration, in practice, consists of focusing the mind upon a given subject, or object, firmly and fixedly, and then holding it there for a certain time, fully intent upon its object, and not allowing itself to be diverted or attracted from its object. It likewise consists in the correlative power of then detaching the mind from that subject, or object, and either allowing it to rest, or else focusing it upon another object. In other words, it either gives undivided attention or else inhibits (or "shuts off") attention from the given subject or object.

To the reader who has had no experience along the lines of mental concentration, it may seem like a very easy mental influence task to focus the mind upon a subject, and then hold it there firmly and fixedly. But a little practice will undeceive such a person and will bring him to a realizing sense of the difficulty of the task. The mind is a very restless thing, and its tendency is to dance from one thing to another, darting here and there, soon tiring of continued attention, and like a spoiled child, seeking a new object upon which to exercise itself.

On the other hand, many people allow their minds to concentrate (involuntarily) upon whatever may strike their fancy, and, forgetting everything else, they give themselves up to the object attracting their attention for the moment, often neglecting duties and important interests, and becoming day dreamers instead of firm thinkers. This involuntary concentration is a thing to be avoided, for it is the allowing of the attention to escape the control of the will. The mental concentration of the occultists is a very different thing, and is solely in control of the will, being applied when desirable, and taken off or inhibited when undesirable.

Trained occultists will concentrate upon a subject or object with a wonderful intensity, seemingly completely absorbed in the subject or object before them, and oblivious to all else in the world. And yet, the task accomplished or the given time expired, they will detach their minds from the object and will be perfectly fresh, watchful and wide-awake to the next matter before them. There is a difference in being controlled by involuntary attention, which is a species of self-hypnotizing, and the control of the attention, which is an evidence of mastery. The secret of mental concentration lies in the control of the attention. And the control of the attention lies in the exercise of the will.

All of the occult authorities begin teaching their pupils *attention* as the first step toward mental concentration. They instruct pupils to examine some familiar object, and endeavor to see as many details as possible in the object. Then after hearing the pupils' reports, the master sends them back to the task, bidding them seek for new details, and so on until at last the pupils have discovered about all concerning the object that can be discovered. The next day a new object is given, and the process is repeated. First simple objects are given, and then more complex ones, until at last objects of great complexity are easily mastered. In this way not only is the power of close observation highly developed, but also the faculty of *attention* becomes so highly strengthened that the pupils are able to exert the greatest amount of mental concentration with scarcely the consciousness of effort. Such people then become giants in the manifestation of mental influence for they are able to mold their minds until they have focused and directed a mighty degree of mental influence toward the desired object.

Among the practices imposed upon their pupils by occult masters may be named mathematics, drawing, analysis, etc. You will readily see why this is. To begin with, mathematics requires the undivided attention of the students—unless they concentrates upon the examples, they will not be able to work out their solution. And, according to the principle in nature that "practice makes perfect," and that "exercise develops power," the practice of the mind along lines requiring voluntary attention and mental concentration will inevitably result in the acquirement of the mental control and power, which renders possible the strongest manifestation of mental influence.

Those who use mental influence must certainly possess the power of focusing the force to a common point, in order to manifest the greatest amount of power and influence. And that faculty of focusing results from the training of the mind along the lines of concentration. And concentration arises from the mastery of voluntary attention. So there you have the whole matter in a nutshell. So your first step toward acquiring mental influence should be to cultivate voluntary attention.

We might fill page after page with exercises designed to strengthen your faculty of voluntary attention, but what would be the use? The best plan is to set you to work to find something upon which to concentrate, for the very search will develop attention. Look around you for some object to study in detail. Then concentrate your attention upon it until you have seen all there is about it to be seen, then take up another object and pursue the practice further.

Take a page—this page, if you will, and count the number of words on it. Then see how many words are required to fill each line, on an average, then see how many letters there are in each word, in each line, on the whole page. Then go over the page and see if any words are misspelled, or if any of the letters are imperfect, etc. In short, get acquainted with this page, until you know all about it. Then take up another page, and after studying it in the same way, compare the two. And so on. Of course this will be very dry and tedious unless you take an interest in it. And, remembering just what the exercise is designed for may arouse this interest. After practicing this way for a short time each day, you will begin to find that you are able to bestow greater attention upon objects upon which you are trying to manifest mental influence. You are developing concentration, and that is the great secret of the use of mental influence.

Key Points

The occult masters have ever impressed upon their pupils the importance and necessity of acquiring the power of mental concentration. The student of mental influence should devote much thought, time and practice to this most important branch of the subject.

Mental concentration consists of focusing the mind upon a given subject, or object, firmly and fixedly, and then holding it—not allowing itself to be diverted or attracted from its object. It likewise consists in the correlative power of then detaching the mind from that subject, or object, and either allowing it to rest, or else focusing it upon another object.

The secret of mental concentration lies in the control of the attention. And the control of the *attention* lies in the exercise of the *will*.

Those who use mental Influence must certainly possess the power of focusing the force to a common point, in order to manifest the greatest amount of power and influence. And that faculty of focusing results from the training of the mind along the lines of concentration. And concentration arises from the mastery of voluntary attention.

CHAPTER 5
MENTAL IMAGING

In our last chapter we called your attention to the first of the two principal factors in the manifestation of mental influence, namely, *Mental Concentration*. In the present chapter we shall consider the second factor tending to render possible the said manifestation, namely, *Mental Imaging*.

What is known as a *mental image*, in occultism, is the mental creation, in the imagination of a "picture" of the things, events or conditions that one desires to be manifested or, materialized in actual effect. A moment's thought will show you that unless you know "just what" you desire, you can take no steps toward attaining it on any plane of manifestation. And the more clearly your desires are perceived in your imagination, the clearer is the work of proceeding toward the realization of that desire. A mental image gives you a framework upon which to work. It is like the drawing of the architect, or the map of the explorer.

Think over this for a few moments until you get the idea firmly fixed in your mind.

The same rule holds well on the plane in which the manifestation of mental influence takes place. Occultists first build up, in their imagination, a mental image or picture of the conditions they wishes to bring about, and then by concentrating their influence strongly, instead of in a haphazard way as is the case with the majority of people who do not understand the laws and principles underlying the manifestations of the forces of mind. The mental image gives shape and direction to the forces, which is being concentrated upon the desired object or subject. It may be compared to the image on the glass of a slide projector through which the focused rays of the lamp pass, the result being that a corresponding image is reproduced upon the screen or curtain beyond. The analogy is a very close one indeed, if we remember that the minds of the majority of people are more or less blank screens or curtains upon which play the pictures produced there by outside influences, suggestions, environments, etc., for very few people realize their individuality, and are merely reflections of the thoughts and ideas of other people.

A visual image is the most perfect form of mental representation whatever the shape, position and relations of objects to space are concerned. The best workers are those who visualize the whole of what they propose to do before they take a tool in their hands. Strategists, artists of all denominations, physicists who contrive new experiments, and in short, all who do not follow routine, have a need for it. A faculty that is of importance in all technical and artistic occupations, that gives accuracy to our perceptions and justice to our generalizations, is starved by lazy disuse instead of being cultivated judiciously in such a way as will, on the whole, bring the best return. A serious study of the best way of developing and utilizing this faculty, without prejudice to the practice of abstract thought in symbols, is one of the many pressing desires in the yet unformed science of education.

This is also true of the manifestations on the mental plane. The clearer a mental picture you possess of anything that you want—the better you know just what you want—and the better you know the latter, the better able you are to take steps to get it. Many people go through life wanting "something," but not really knowing "just what" they do want. Is it any wonder that they do not realize or materialize their desires any better?

The same thing holds well on the plane of manifestation of mental influence. If you wish to materialize anything by the use of the influence, it is necessary to have a mental image of just what you want to materialize, by creating a mental "pattern" or plan, in the shape of a mental picture, through and around which you may direct his thought-currents.

The occultists manifesting the greatest degree of mental influence acquire by practice this art of creating mental images of that which they wish to materialize. They train their imagination in this way until the very act of creating the mental image acts strongly toward the actual materialization or event, as "actually existing" in their minds before they attempt to concentrate their thought-waves upon the task of accomplishing it. Then the mental picture, being completed and standing in strong outline, they focus their mental force through it, just as in the case of the slide projector before referred to, and the picture is reproduced on the screen of mentality of other people.

The imagination may be strengthened in many ways, the principle being constant and persistent practice. The practice of recalling to the memory of scenes previously witnessed, and then describing them to others or else drawing a rough picture of them will help in this matter. Describe to others scenes that you have witnessed, occurrences, details of appearances, and so on until you are able to reproduce mentally the aspects and appearances of the things. Then you may begin to draw mental pictures of things desired as if they were being drawn on the screen of your mind. See, mentally, the things as actually occurring—create a little playhouse of your own, in your mind, and there enact the plays that you wish to witness in actual life. When you have acquired this, you will be able to project your mental pictures on the screen of objectivity in actual life with far greater effect.

In thinking of this subject, you would do well to remember the illustration of the slide projector, for the figure is a good one, and will enable you to carry the idea better in your mind. You see, in giving you this suggestion, we are really telling you to form a mental picture of the mental slide projector, using the illustration given—you see how much easier it is for you to think of it in this way and how much easier it is for you to manifest it in practice.

Build your mental images by degrees, commencing with the general outlines, and then filling in the details. Always commence by trying simple and easy things, and then working up to the more complex.

Caution: Do not allow your imagination to "run away with you"—do not become a dreamer of dreams and a doer of nothing. You must master your imagination and make it your servant and not your master. You must make it do your bidding, instead of allowing it to dictate to you.

You will see in the succeeding chapters the important part that mental imaging plays in the different phases of mental influence. Even when it is not referred to directly by name, you will see that the "idea" sought to be conveyed by one mind to another—the feeling, desire or mental state sought to be transferred from one mind to others—must and does depend very materially for strength upon the dearness and completeness of the mental image held in the mind of the person seeking to do the influencing, the "projector" of the mental image upon the screen of the minds of others. Carry this principle well in mind that you may see its operation in the different forms.

Key Points

Mental image is the mental creation, the imagination of a "picture" of the things, events or conditions that one desires to be manifested or, materialized in actual effect. Unless you know "just what" you desire, you can take no steps toward attaining it on any plane of manifestation. And the more clearly your desires are perceived in your imagination, the clearer is the work of proceeding toward the realization of that desire. A mental image gives you a framework upon which to work.

The clearer a mental picture you possess of any-thing that you want—the better you know just what you want—and the better you know the latter, the better able you are to take steps to get it.

Build your mental images by degrees, commenc-ing with the general outlines, and then filling in the details. Always commence by trying simple and easy things, and then working up to the more complex and difficult feats.

CHAPTER 6

FASCINATION

In this and the next chapter we shall present to you information regarding the effect of Mental Influence manifested when there is personal contact between the persons using the power and the person affected. Then we shall pass on to a consideration of the effect produced when the persons are not in direct contact with each other.

There are two general forms of the direct use of mental influence, which, although somewhat resembling each other, may still be separated into two classes. The first is called *fascination* and the second *hypnotism*.

Fascination is the manifestation of mental influence when the two persons are together, without passes or the usual hypnotic methods. *Hypnotism* is the use of the power, also, when the two parties are together, but accompanied by passes or hypnotic methods.

Under the head of fascination are to be found the manifestations generally known as *personal magnetism*, *charm*,
or *charisma*. Many persons, often without their conscious
knowledge of the principles employed, quite commonly
employ these, in varying degrees. Many persons are possessed of the power of fascination "naturally" and without
having studied or practiced the principles. Many others, not
originally possessing the power, have acquired by study and
practice the power to influence people in this way. For, it
must be known, the power may be acquired by study and
practice just as may any other power of mind and body. To
some it is easy, to others difficult—but all may acquire a very
great degree of the power by intelligent study and practice
of the underlying principles.

Fascination is one of the oldest forms of the manifestations
of mental influence. It was known to, and employed by, the
earliest humans. It is even found among the lower animals
that pursue their prey or capture their mates by its use. It has
been defined as acting upon by some powerful or irresistible influence; influencing by an irresistible charm; alluring,
exciting, irresistibly or powerfully, charming, captivating or
attracting powerfully, influencing the imagination, reason
or will of another in an uncontrollable manner; enchanting,
captivating or alluring, powerfully or irresistibly.

As we have just said, this power is observable even among
the lower animals in some cases. Instances are related by
naturalists, which scorpions have fascinated other insects,
causing them to circle around and around until finally the
insect would plunge down right within striking distance

of the scorpion, which would then devour its prey. Birds of prey unquestionably fascinate their game, and people who have been brought in contact with wild tigers, lions, etc., have testified that they felt paralyzed in some manner, their legs refusing to obey their will, and their minds seeming to become numbed and stunned. Those who have seen a mouse in the presence of a cat will testify to the effect of some power exerted by the latter. Birds in the presence of a cat and serpents also manifest symptoms of a conquered will. And naturalists cite many instances of the employment of this force by birds seeking to captivate and charm their mates at the beginning of the season.

It has been noticed that certain individuals possess this power to a great degree. Some of the "great people" of ancient and modem times having been so filled with the power that they could manage their followers almost as one would move automatons. Julius Caesar had this power developed to a great degree, and used it from youth to his last days. His soldiers—who would undertake almost any task at his bidding, worshiped him—almost as a god. Napoleon also possessed this charm to a wonderful degree. It enabled him to control men with whom he came in contact, and to bend them to his will. He rose from a poor student to the dignity and power of the Emperor of France. When banished to Elba he escaped, and landing in France, alone and unarmed, confronted the ranks of the French army drawn up to capture him, and walking towards the soldiers compelled the latter to throw down their guns and flock to his support. He entered Paris at the head of the great army, which had been sent forth to capture him. This is no wild legend, but a sober fact of history. And in our own times we see how certain leaders sweep people before them and move them around like pawns on the chessboard of life.

All of the above mentioned phenomena comes under the head of *fascination*, and is the result of the emanation of streams of active thought-waves from the mind of a person, the same being strongly concentrated and directed toward those whom the person wishes to affect. The person forms a strong thought in his or her mind and sends it out to the others charged with the force of concentrated will, so that the other person feels it most strongly and forcibly. The fundamental idea is the forming of the thought, and then sending it out to the other person.

For instance, if you wish a person to like you, you should form in your mind this thought: "That person likes me," fixing it in your own mind as a fact. Then project to him or her the concentrated thought, "You like me—you like me very much," with an air of assurance and confidence. The other person is bound to feel the effect unless he or she has acquired a knowledge of the subject and is using self-protection. The thought should be sent forth with the strength that usually accompanies a strong spoken statement, but you must not actually "speak" the words aloud—you should merely say them strongly "in your mind."

If you wish to produce an effect or impress strength upon another person, the same process may be used, changing the thought and vibrations to the idea that you have a stronger will than the other person, and are able to overcome that person's will—using the silent message of "I am Stronger than you—my will overcomes yours."

Some successful salespeople use the following method in reaching their customers. They form a thought that the other person desires their goods very much, and then they send out the thought-waves that "You desire my goods—you want them very much—you have an irresistible longing for them."

Others use the following when they wish another to comply with their wishes: "You will do as I say—*will do as I say*—you will yield to me fully and completely," or words to that effect.

You will readily see from the above examples that the whole principle employed in any and all of these cases consists of *fascination*, and is the result of the emanation of streams of active thought-waves from the mind of a person being strongly concentrated and directed toward those whom the person wishes to affect. The person forms a strong thought in his or her mind and sends it out to the others charged with the force of concentrated will, so that the other person feels it most strongly and forcibly. The fundamental idea is the forming of the thought, and then sending it out to the other person.

In short,

(1) The thought of what the person wishes the other to do is held firmly in the mind; and

(2) That thought is projected to the other, silently, in the shape of unspoken words.

In the above you have the whole secret of *fascination* condensed to a small space. You will understand of course, that the words are only a means of concentrating and vitalizing the thought. Animals merely feel desires, but are able to fascinate by the strength of them, although they cannot use words. And one person may fascinate others without understanding a word of their language, the real strength coming from the strength of the desire behind the words. The formation of the desire-thought into words, is merely for the purpose of concentrating and focusing the thought, for words are concentrated symbols of ideas, thoughts or feelings.

The exact process of "sending forth" the thought-wave to the other is difficult to describe. You know how you feel when you say something very forcible and emphatic to another person. You can fairly "feel" the force of the words being hurled at the other person. Well, cultivate that same power in sending forth the "unspoken word" in the above manner, and you will soon be able to notice the effect of the thought on the other. It may help you to imagine that you can see the force flying from you to the other. The imagination properly used helps very much in these matters, for it creates a mental path over which the force may travel.

You must not act awkwardly when sending out the thought-waves, but converse in an ordinary manner, sending your thought-waves between your speeches, when the other person is talking to you, or at any pause in the conversation. It is always well to send first a powerful thought-wave before the conversation is opened, preferably while you are approaching the person. And it is likewise well to terminate the interview with a "parting shot" of considerable strength. You will find that these thought-waves are of far greater power than spoken words, and then again, you can in this way send out impressions that you could not utter in spoken words for obvious reasons.

This may explain how you have been affected by persons who have influenced you at times in your past life. Now that you know the secret you will be in a measure immune from further impressions from others. And when you read the concluding chapter, entitled "Self-Protection," you will be able to surround yourself with a protective armor through which the thought-waves cannot penetrate, but which will turn aside the shafts directed toward you.

Key Points

Fascination is the manifestation of mental influence when the two persons are together, without passes or the usual hypnotic methods. *Hypnotism* is the use of the power, also, when the two parties are together, but accompanied by passes or hypnotic methods.

Fascination is one of the oldest forms of the manifestations of mental influence. It consists of acting upon by some powerful or irresistible influence, an irresistible, powerful, force, influencing the imagination, reason or will of another in an uncontrollable manner.

Fascination is the result of the emanation of streams of active thought-waves from the mind of a person are concentrated and directed toward those whom the person wishes to affect.

(1) The thought of what you wish the other to do is held firmly in the mind; and

(2) That thought is projected to the other, silently, in the shape of unspoken words.

CHAPTER 7
HYPNOTIC INFLUENCE

As mentioned in the previous chapter, there is a general resemblance between the manifestation of mental influence, known as *fascination*, and that known as *hypnotic influence*. In the manifestation known as fascination, the influence is exerted solely by thought-waves passing from mind to mind without a physical medium or channel other than the atmosphere. In *Hypnotic influence*, on the contrary, the influence is heightened by means of passes, stroking or eye contact.

In hypnotic influence the mind of the person affected, whom we shall call the "subject," is rendered passive by a flow of mental energy calculated to make the subject more or less drowsy or sleepy, and therefore less calculated to set up powers of resistance to the thought-waves of the person using the influence. But the power employed is the same in all cases, no matter whether they fall under the classification of fascination or whether that of hypnotic influence.

The two classes of manifestation, as a matter of fact, really blend into each other, and it is difficult to draw a dividing line in some cases.

Hypnotic influence is a form of that which was formerly termed *mesmerism*, which name was given to it in honor of its discoverer, Frederick Anton Mesmer, who practiced this form of mental influence during the latter half of the eighteenth century. As a fact, however, the force and its use was known to the ancients centuries ago. Mesmer merely rediscovered it.

Mesmer taught that the power was based upon the presence of a strange universal fluid which pervaded everything, and which had a peculiar effect upon the nerves and brains of people. He and his followers believed that it was necessary to put the subjects into a sound sleep before they could be influenced. But both of these ideas have given way to the new theories on the subject now held by investigators and students of the subject.

It is now known that the "magnetic fluid" believed in by Mesmer and his followers is nothing else than the currents of thought-waves emanating from the mind of the operator. And it is also known that the deep sleep condition, although it sometimes facilitates the process, is not necessary to render the will of the subject subservient to that of the operator.

It is also now known that the nerves of the arms and fingers afford a highly sensitive conductor for the mental currents, which may be propelled over them to the mind of the subjects, or to their nerves and muscles. This fact is explained by the well-known scientific fact that the material of which the nerves are composed is almost identical with that of the brain—in fact the nervous system may be spoken of as a continuation of the brain itself. It is now also known that the eye has a peculiar property of transmitting the mental currents along the rays of light entering it and from thence to the eyes of the other person. The above fact explains the phenomena of hypnotic influence, as it is now known to science. The question of *suggestion* also has a bearing on the subject.

Modern operators do not produce the "deep sleep" condition usually except in cases when it is desired to produce some form of psychic phenomena apart from the subject of mental influence—that is, in which they are merely inducing the deep hypnotic condition in order to get the subject into a psychic condition in which the phenomena mentioned may be manifested or exhibited. We shall not enter into this phase of the subject in this book for it is outside of the immediate subject. Modern hypnotic investigators merely induce a passive state in the mind, nerves or muscles of the subject sufficient to reduce the powers of resistance, and then give orders or "verbal suggestions" accompanied by a projection of their thought-waves into the mind of the subject.

In order to illustrate the subject, here are a few experiments, which may be easily performed by anyone manifesting the power of concentration and thought-projection. There is of course a great difference in the degrees of impressionability of different persons to hypnotic influence—that is to say, difference in degrees of resistance. Some persons will interpose a strong resistance, while others will sct up a very feeble resistance, which is easily beaten down by the will of the operator. In the following experiments it is best to begin by getting some person who is perfectly willing for the experiment, and who will not interpose a resistance but who is willing to become passive—a person friendly to you and interested in the experiments.

Let us say that you have chosen your sister to be your subject. Begin by having her stand before you. Then make sweeping passes in front of her from head to foot. Then make a few passes in front of her face, then along her arms. Then take hold of her hands and hold them a little while, looking her straight in the eyes. Make all passes downward. Avoid levity or laughter and maintain a serious, earnest expression and frame of mind.

Then standing in front of your sister, tell her to take her will off of her legs and stand perfectly passive and relaxed. Then looking her straight in the eyes, say to her: "Now, I am going to draw you forward toward me by my mental power—you will feel yourself falling forward toward me—don't resist but let yourself come toward me—I will catch you, don't be afraid—now come—come—come—now you're coming, that's right," You may repeat this several times. You will find that she will begin to sway toward you and in a moment or two will fall forward in your arms. It is unnecessary to say that you should concentrate your mind steadily upon the idea of her falling forward, using your will firmly to that effect. It will help matters if you hold your hands on each side of her head, but just in front of her, not touching her, however, and then draw away your hands, toward yourself, saying at the same time: "Come now come—you're coming," etc. Standing behind the subject and drawing her backward may reverse this experiment. Be sure and catch her in your arms when she fails to protect her from a fall to the floor.

In the same manner you may fasten her hands together, telling her that she cannot draw them apart. Or you may start her revolving her hands, and then giving her orders that she cannot stop them. Or you may draw her all around the room after you, following your finger that you have pointed at her nose. Or you may make her experience a feeling of heat and pain by touching your finger to her hand and telling her that it is hot.

All of the familiar simple experiments may be performed successfully upon a large percentage of persons, in this way, by following the above general directions. This book will not go into detail of the higher experiments of hypnotism, as that forms a special subject by itself. The above experiments are given merely for the purpose of showing you that the phenomena of hypnotic influence does not require any "magic," and is all explainable upon the hypothesis of mental influence by means of thought- waves and mental induction.

In the above experiments, be sure you "take off" the influence afterward, by making upward passes, and send strong thought-waves that the influence pass off. Do not neglect this.

In your experiments, you will soon discover the power of your eye upon the other persons. You will be able to almost feel the force passing from your gaze to theirs. And this is true in the case of the passes and stroking of the hands. You will feel the vibratory waves flowing from your hands into their nervous system. It is wonderful what power is aroused in a person after conducting a few experiments along these lines.

And now a word of warning—Beware of people who are always putting their hands on you, or patting or stroking you, or wishing to hold your hands a long time. Many persons do this from force of habit, and innocently, but others do so with the intention of producing a mild form of hypnotic influence upon you. If you meet such persons, and find them attempting anything of this sort, you can counteract their influence by sending them a strong thought current (as stated in the last chapter), sending them the thought: "You *cannot* affect me—I am too strong for you—you *cannot* play your tricks on me." It is a good plan to practice this counteracting force when you are shaking hands with a "magnetic" person who seems to affect people. You will soon be able to distinguish these people by a certain force about them and a peculiar expression in their eyes, at the same time using your protective will upon them.

Caution young girls against allowing young men to be too free in using their hands in caressing them, and a word of advice to young men in your family would not be out of place in this respect. There are many cases of sex-attraction, leading to very deplorable results, arising from a conscious or unconscious use of this simple form of hypnotic influence. The danger lies in the fact that it renders one passive to other influences, and more readily led into temptation and to yield to the desires or will of the other person. A word to the wise should be sufficient. The use of this power for immoral purposes is a terrible crime and brings down upon the user deplorable results, which all occultists know and teach. All people should learn to resist such influences when exerted upon them. Forewarned is forearmed.

Key Points

Modern hypnotic investigators merely induce a passive state in the mind, nerves or muscles of the subject sufficient to reduce the powers of resistance, and then give orders or "verbal suggestions" accompanied by a projection of their thought-waves into the mind of the subject.

With a little experimenting in using this technique, you will soon discover the power of your eye upon the other persons. You will be able to almost feel the force passing from your gaze to theirs. And this is true in the case of the passes and stroking of the hands. You will feel the vibratory waves flowing from your hands into their nervous system. It is wonderful what power is aroused.

Beware of people who are always putting their hands on you, or patting or stroking you, or wishing to hold your hands a long time. Many persons do this from force of habit, and innocently, but others do so with the intention of producing a mild form of hypnotic influence upon you. You can counteract their influence by sending them a strong thought current sending them the thought: "You *cannot* affect me—I am too strong for you—you *cannot* play your tricks on me."

CHAPTER 8
INFLUENCING AT A DISTANCE

In the two preceding chapters you learned about the manifestation of mental influence when the user or projector of the force was in actual contact with, or in presence of, the person or persons he or she was aiming to influence. In this chapter, and the one immediately following it, you will learn about the manifestation of the influence when the persons affected are removed in space from the person using the influence.

The general public is familiar in a general way with the phenomena of hypnotism and to a lesser degree with the phenomena of fascination in its more common forms of personal magnetism, etc. But as regards the use of the influence at a distance people are more or less skeptical owing to a lack of knowledge of the subject. And still every day new facts and instances of such an influence are discovered. The teaching of various cults along these lines is now awakening a new interest in the subject, and a desire to learn something regarding the laws and principles underlying the same.

As strange as it may appear at first glance, the principles underlying mental influence at a distance are precisely the same as those underlying the use of influence when the persons are in the presence of each other. A little thought must show the truth of this. In the case of present influence the mental-currents flow across an intervening space between the two minds—there is a space outside of the two minds to be traversed by the currents. And a moment's thought will show you that the difference between present influence and distant influence is merely a matter of degree—a question of a little more or less space to be traversed by the currents.

This being so, it follows that the methods used must be identical. Of course, in the case of personal influence the added effect of the voice, manner, suggestive methods, the eye, etc., are present, which render the result more easily obtained, and causes the "rapport" condition to be more easily established. But with this exception the methods are identical, and even the advantages accruing from the exception mentioned may be duplicated by practice and development in the case of distant influence.

There are a number of methods given by the authorities in this matter of distant influencing, but they are all based upon the same principles named in the previous chapters of this book, i.e. vibrations, thought-waves, mental induction, concentration and mental imaging—in these words you have the key to the subject—the rest is all a matter of practice and development, and variation.

One of the most elementary, and yet one of the most effective methods known to occultists is that of creating a mental image of the person "treated" (for that is the common term among modern writers on the subject) in the sense of imagining the subject to be seated in a chair in front of the person treating him or her at a distance. The treator proceeds to give both verbal commands, and at the same time directs thought-waves toward this imaginary person. This process establishes a psychic condition between the treator and the actual person, although the latter may be removed from the treator by many miles of space. This was the method of the ancient magicians and wonder-workers, and has always been a favorite among persons pursuing these experiments, of desirous, of mentally influencing others at a distance.

A variation of the above, very common in former days, was to mold a clay or wax figure, calling it by the name of the person treated, and identifying it in the mind and imagination with the other person. A variation is also noticed in the cases where a photograph, lock of hair, article of clothing, etc., is used in this way as a psychic connecting link between the two persons. The practitioners of black magic, witchcraft and of nefarious perversions of mental influence seemed to prefer these methods, although, on the contrary, they are used with the very best results today by many in giving beneficial treatments to absent patients, friends and others whose welfare is desired. The only effect the mental image of the person, or the picture, etc., has is the fact that by these means a psychic connection link is set up along which the thought-waves travel more readily.

In the above forms of treatment the treator treats the mental image, picture, etc., precisely as if the person were actually present. For the time being it is forgotten that the person may be hundreds of miles away, and the influence of the treator is on the image, or picture, etc., because the latter is really the starting point of the psychic chain, which leads direct to the person. The treator sends thought-waves toward the object, and in some cases actually talks (mentally) to the person by means of the medium mentioned. The treator may give commands, arguments, remonstrance, persuasion, etc., just as if the person were actually present. In short, the treator acts as if the person was actually present and receptive to the influence projected.

Another way, employed by some, is to begin darting thought-waves toward the other person, forming in the imagination a gradual lengthening "psychic-wire" composed of thought-vibrations. Those practicing this form state that when the psychic-wire is projected sufficiently far (and it travels with incredible speed) and comes in contact with the mind of the other person, the treator feels at once that contact has been established by a peculiar faint "shock" similar to that of a very mild galvanic current. Then the treator proceeds to send thought-currents along the psychic-wire in the same manner as if the person were actually present, as described under the head of *fascination*, in a preceding chapter. In fact, such treatments, and the others mentioned in this chapter, are really and practically "long distance fascination."

Another form of distant treatment consists in forming an "astral-tube," The astral-tube is set up in a similar manner to the "psychic-wire," and projected toward the person desired to influence. It is formed in the imagination as a "vortex-ring," similar to the little ring of smoke puffed out by the cigar smoker, only larger—about six inches to one foot wide—or, better still, like the ring of smoke ejected from the stack of a locomotive sometimes when it is puffing rapidly. This vortex-ring is then seen, in the imagination, by the use of the will, to lengthen out in the shape of a tube, which rapidly extends and travels toward the person treated, in a manner identical with that of the psychic-wire. This tube is known to occultists as the "astral-tube," and is employed in various forms of occult and psychic phenomena, such as clairvoyance. Those following this method of distant influencing report that they recognize the completion of the tube by a sensation of stoppage and a feeling of "rapport" having been established between themselves and the other person. In some cases they report that they are able to faintly "see" the figure of the other person in miniature at the other end of the tube. The tube once established the treatment is proceeded with as if they were in the actual presence of the person treated. In many respects the "psychic-wire" and the "astral-tube" methods are similar, and a statement concerning one is generally true of the other.

There are two other methods frequently used in distant influencing which we shall now briefly describe.

The first of these two methods consists in sitting or standing in a quiet place, or rather in some place in which you can concentrate (the advanced occultist can find peace in the midst of the noise) and then directing your thought-waves toward the other person, forming in the imagination a mental picture of the force flying from you toward the other, like tiny sparks of electricity, or of a subtle fluid. This mental picture tends to give a concentrative force to the current, which renders them powerful, and sends them direct to the desired spot.

The second of these two methods is that used by the most advanced occultists who have advanced beyond the use of the methods described just now. These people simply stand or sit quietly and concentrate their minds until they attain the state of mental calm known to many as "the silence." Then they create a strong mental picture of the person treated, surrounded by the conditions desired created, or doing the things desired to be done. This is one of the highest forms of mental influence and really approaches a higher phase of influence than that of the mental plane as generally known. A picture of a person held in the mind in this way—the person being seen in perfect, robust health, and happy and successful—tends to materialize the same conditions in the person in real life. This form of treatment, however, is possible only to those of great concentration, and who have mastered the act of mental imaging, and who also possess creative willpower to a marked degree. Some degree of success in it, however, is open to nearly every student who practices along these lines.

Before practicing any of these experiments, read what we have said in the chapter on "Magic Black and White," and guard against employing the power for evil purposes, for the fate of the "Black Magician" is a sad one.

Key Points

The principles underlying mental influence at a distance are precisely the same as those underlying the use of influence when the persons are in the presence of each other.

One of the most elementary, and yet one of the most effective methods known to occultists is that of creating a mental image of the person "treated" in the sense of imagining the subject to be seated in a chair in front of the person treating him or her at a distance. The treator proceeds to give both verbal commands, and at the same time directs thought-waves toward this imaginary person. This process establishes a psychic condition between the treator and the actual person, although the latter may be removed from the treator by many miles of space.

CHAPTER 9

INFLUENCING "EN MASSE"

In the last chapter the manifestation of mental influence at a distance was considered in so far as was concerned the influencing of one or more persons by another. There is another phase of the subject that must not be overlooked, and that is the influencing of large numbers of people by some active, strong projector of mental influence. This form of the manifestation of the power is known as *Mental Influencing En Masse*—"En masse," of course, means "in a body"—or "in a crowd," and mental influencing en masse means the use of the influence in the phase of exerting a strong attracting or directing power to the mind of "the crowd," or rather, "the public, or a large number of people."

This form of the use of the power is that consciously or unconsciously exerted by the great leaders in the fields of statesmanship, politics, business, finance or military life.

You will at once recall a number of the so called "great lead-ers" of history from ancient times down to our own times who seemed to exert a wonderfully, almost miraculous, effect upon the minds of the people, causing people to see things through their eyes and to carry out their ideals, will or desires. On a smaller scale are the majority of the suc-cessful people who depend upon public support. In fact, this influence in some degree is used by nearly all who suc-ceed in any form of business or profession, in which success calls for the attraction of other people toward the occupa-tion of the person in question. This may seem like a strange thought to many, but occultists know it as the truth, not-withstanding.

The most common form of *influencing en masse* is the same as that manifested by a majority of people by reason of their desire for the success of certain things. By desire we do not mean the mere "wanting" or "wishing" state of mind, but rather that eager longing, craving, demanding mental state that evinces a hungry reaching out for the desired thing. You will notice that the men and women who "get things" are generally those who are possessed of a strong, burning desire for the things in question, which prompts them to be more aggressive in the search for satisfaction of the desire possessing them. These people are constantly sending out strong waves of thought-vibrations, which has a drawing, attracting influence upon all with whom they come in con-tact, and tending to draw such persons toward the center of attraction, which is, of course, the mind of the person send-ing out such thoughts. In the same way people possessed of a strong fear of a thing will send out similar attracting waves, which have a tendency to attract or draw to them the people calculated to bring about the materialization of the thing feared.

This may sound paradoxical, but the secret lies in the fact that in both the case of desire and fear the mind forms the mental image, which tends to become materialized. Fear, after all, is a form of "expectation," which, alas, too, often tends to materialize it. "The thing that I have feared, hath come upon me," says Job, and in that saying he has stated the experience of humankind. The way to fight things you may fear is to create a burning desire for the opposite thing.

Other persons who have either studied the principles of mental influence, or else have stumbled upon certain facts concerning the same, improve upon this elementary form of *influencing in masse* just mentioned. They send out the thought-waves consciously and deliberately, erecting the mental image, and holding strongly to it, so that in time their sweeps of mental currents reach further and further away and bring a greater number of people under the influence and into the field of attraction. They "treat" the public "en masse" by holding the strong mental picture of that which they desire, and then sending out strong thought-currents of desire in all directions, willing that those coming within their radius shall be attracted toward the ideas expressed in the mental image projected in all directions.

The constant dwelling upon some special object or subject, by those who have developed concentration, strong wills and fixity of purpose, has the effect of sending out from the mind of those people great circles, constantly widening, of thought-waves, which sweep ever outward like waves in a pond caused by dropping in a stone. These waves reach and affect a great number of people, and will render them at least "interested" in the object or subject thought of, and the indifference has been overcome. Other appeals to the minds of these people will be far more likely to reach them than otherwise, for "interest" is the first step toward attention, and attention is another step toward action.

Of course, there are very many people sending out circles of thought-waves, and these currents come in contact with each other and tend to neutralize each. But now and then a particularly strong person will send out waves that will persist even after meeting other currents, and will reach the minds of the public in spite of the opposition. These thought-currents have the personality of the senders, and reflect the character of their wills, be it strong or weak. The mental influence sent out by a strong retailer in a town will soon make itself felt in a subtle manner, and the store becomes a center of attractive influence, although the public does no understand just why. In the same way some lawyers spring into public favor, although not possessing greater ability than other lawyers. And popular preachers make their influence felt in a community in similar ways, although often they are not conscious of just what force they are using. Their only knowledge of this is that they have a feeling of inward strength and an attractive influence over people, and at the same time a burning ardent desire to draw people their way, and a strong will to back it up with. And these are just the mental qualities that create and manifest the strongest kind of mental influence. And besides, these people almost invariably "know just what they want"—there is no mere vague "wishing" about them—they make a clear mental picture of the things that they wish to bring about, and then they bend every effort toward materializing the picture. Everything they do towards accomplishing their ends gives an additional impetus to their constantly widening and constantly strengthening circle of power and influence.

Some masters of this art of influencing the public create a mental picture of themselves sending out great volumes of thought-waves for a time, and then afterward mentally imparting a rotary motion to the waves, until at last they form a mental whirlpool rushing round and round and always sucking in toward the center. An effort of this kind acts on the mental plane just as a physical whirlpool acts on the physical plane, that is it draws into its power all that comes in contact with its force. This is one of the most powerful forms of *influencing en masse*, and is used with great effect by many of the leaders of this age; who have acquainted themselves fully with the secrets of the ancient occultists. Ancient occultism and modern finance seem far apart, but they are really working together to further the interests of some of these powerful minds of the day—and the public is paying the bill.

You will readily see from what has been said that people who have cultivated the faculty of concentration and have acquired the art of creating sharp, clear, strong mental images, and who when engaged in an undertaking will so charge their minds with the idea of success, will be bound to become an attracting center. If such people will keep this mental picture ever in their minds, even though it may be in the background of their minds, when they are attending to the details and planning of their affairs—if they will give this mental picture a prominent place in their mental gallery, taking a frequent glance at it, and using their will upon it to create new scenes of actual success, they will create for themselves a center of radiating thought that will surely be felt by those coming within its field of influence.

Such people frequently "see" people coming to them and their enterprises and falling in line with their plans. They mentally "see" money flowing in to them, and all of their plans working out right. In short, they mentally imagine each step of their plans a little ahead of the time for their execution and concentrate forcibly and earnestly upon them. It is astonishing to witness how events, people, circumstances and things seem to move in place in actual life as if urged by some mighty power to serve to materialize the conditions so imaged in the mind of these people. But, understood, there has got to be active mental effort behind the imaging. Daydreamers do not materialize thought—they merely dissipate energy. People, who convert thought in activity and material being, throw energy into the task and put forth their willpower through the picture on the slide. Without the rays of the will there will be no picture projected, no matter how beautifully the imagination has pictured it. Thoughts pictured in mental images and then vitalized by the force of the desire and will tend to objectify themselves into material beings.

Key Points

Mental influencing en masse means the use of the influence in the phase of exerting a strong attracting or directing power to the mind of "the crowd," or rather, "the public," or a large number of people.

The men and women who "get things" are generally those who are possessed of a strong, burning desire for the things in question, which prompts them to be more of less aggressive in the search for satisfaction of the desire possessing them. These people are constantly sending out strong waves of thought-vibrations, which has a drawing, attracting influence upon all with whom they come in contact, and tending to draw such persons toward the center of attraction, which is, of course, the mind of the person sending out such thoughts.

There are some people who have the power to send out thought-waves consciously and deliberately, erecting the mental image, and holding strongly to it, so that in time their sweeps of mental currents reach further and further away and bring a greater number of people under the influence and into the field of attraction.

People with this power make a clear mental picture of the things that they wish to bring about, and then they bend every effort toward materializing the picture. Everything they do towards accomplishing their ends gives an additional impetus to their constantly widening and constantly strengthening circle of power and influence.

People who have cultivated the faculty of concentration and have acquired the art of creating sharp, clear, strong mental images, and who when engaged in an undertaking will so charge their minds with the idea of success, will be bound to become an attracting center. If such people will keep this mental picture ever in their minds, even though it may be in the background of their minds, taking a frequent glance at it, and using their will upon it to create new scenes of actual success, they will create for themselves a center of radiating thought that will surely be felt by those coming within its field of influence.

CHAPTER 10
THE NEED OF THE KNOWLEDGE

Although the true scientific principles underlying the subject of mental influence have been but recently recognized and taught to the general public, still the knowledge is far from being new. The occultists of the old civilizations undoubtedly understood the underlying principles and used them in practice, thus gaining an ascendancy over the masses. And more than this, the masses themselves had a more or less comprehensive knowledge of the working principles of the subject, for we find among all peoples, in all times, records of the use of this power. Under one name or another—under one form or another—mental influence has been operated and used from the earliest times. And today, even in the most remote portions of the globe, and among the most savage and barbarous peoples we find instances of the employment of this force.

The forms of the manifestation of mental influence are many and varied. In some cases it manifests under the form of a fascinating, attracting power exerted by some people, which causes such persons to draw or attract other persons to them. Persons are allured or "charmed" by others possessing this power, and their affections are taken captive by this mysterious force. Some persons are spoken of as "fascinating," "possessing powers of charming," having "winning ways," having "great personal magnetism," etc. Others exert another form of the power in the driving of and compelling others to do their bidding, and people speak of them as having "a compelling will," being able "to work their will" on those around them, possessing "dominating powers," etc.

We are also brought face to face with the wonderful effects of *mental science* under one form or another, under this name or that term, with the many forms of "treatments" followed by the different schools and cults. Then we read in the pages of history about the mysterious powers recorded under the name of witchcraft, hexes, voodoo's, and black magic, including the Hawaiian "Kahuna" work. And turning back the pages of history to Ancient time, Greece, Persia and Egypt, not to speak of India, ancient and modern, we find innumerable instances of the employment of, and knowledge of, mental influence in some of its forms.

And although many will seek to deny the fact, scientific investigators and students realize that there is but one real underlying principle under and back of all of the various forms of manifestation. The good results, and the evil results, all arise from the employment of the same force, strange as it may appear at first thought. The secret lies in the fact that this mental influence is a great natural force, just as is electricity or any other natural forces, and it may be, and is, used for both good and evil purposes. The electricity which runs out machines, lights our houses and performs countless other beneficent tasks has also been used to electrocute criminals, and the unfortunate person who touches a "live wire" may be struck with instant death. The sun, which warms our earth and renders life possible, also kills countless persons exposed to its rays on the desert, or even in our large cities. Fire, that which has been one of the most potent factors in the evolution of humankind from barbarism to civilization, is also a mighty enemy, destroying both property and lives. Water, that most necessary element, which renders life possible, and which is necessary to grow grain and to perform countless other good services, also acts as an enemy at times, drowning people and sweeping away their homes. Gravitation, which holds all things in place, from suns and stars down to the tiniest atom of matter, also causes people to fall to their death from high places, or brings down on their heads objects from above them. In short, every natural force or power is capable of producing either beneficent or baleful effects according to the circumstances of the case. We recognize these things, and accept them as a law of nature. And yet some would deny the identity of the power of mental influence as manifested in its good and bad uses.

There will be people who ascribe to God all the good qualities of mental influence, and ascribe to the devil all of its evil uses. These people have primitive minds. Their counterparts are seen in those who would credit God with the helpful rain or sun, and who ascribe to the devil the same things when there occurs a flood or a drought. Such reasoning is worthy only of the primitive mind. The forces are natural forces, and work according to their own laws, imminent in their constituent qualities and nature, and are in that sense "above good and evil." When they work for our interest and comfort, we call them "good"—when they work harm and discomfort, we call them "bad"—but the force remains unchanged, being neither "good" nor "bad." And thus it is with the power of mental influence—it is above "good" and "bad"—it is a great natural force, capable of being used either way. But, remember this, there is a difference.

While the force in itself is neither good nor bad the individual who employs it may be, and it is, "good" or "bad," according to its use. Just as a person commits a good act when using a gun to slay a wild beast that is attacking another person, or a bad act when using that gun to shoot another person, so is a person good or bad according to the use of mental influence. The merit or demerit lies in the intention and purpose of the user, not in the force or power employed.

On all sides of us we may see the manifestation of the possession of mental influence. We see people who are able to sway those around them in some mysterious and wonderful way, either by their powers of persuasion of by their dominant will power. Some spring into prominence and power suddenly, in a way unaccountable to those who are ignorant of the secret of mental influence. Certain people seem to have "something about them" that makes them attractive or successful in their relations with other people. The "personal magnetism" of leaders manifests itself strongly, some having this power to such an extent that the masses follow them like a great flock of sheep.

We have all come in contact with the salesperson who managed in some way to sell us things that we did not want and had no use for, and afterwards we wondered and wondered how it all happened. If we had but understood the laws of mental influence this could not have happened. We have all felt ourselves, at some time or another in our lives, in the presence of individuals who almost compelled us to do what we knew in our hearts we should not do. Knowledge of the laws of mental influence would have enabled us to overcome the temptation.

And not only in the case of personal interviews have we been affected. There is a far more subtle and dangerous use of the power, i.e., in the shape of "distant influence," or "absent treatment," as it had been called. And the increase in the interest and knowledge of occult matters has resulted in a widely diffused knowledge of this great force, and its consequent employment, worthily and unworthily, by many people who are thereby enabled to gain an influence over others, who are not familiar with the laws of the force. It would surprise many people if they knew that some of the multi-millionaires of the country, and some of its greatest politicians and leaders, were secret students of occultism, and who were using their forces upon the masses of the people.

Not only this, but there are schools of occultism which teach their pupils the theory, practice and art of mental influence, under one name or another—under this guise or that—the result being that there are a greater number of people equipped for the use of this force and instructed in the practice of employing it turned out every year than is generally imagined. There are schools in the techniques of selling that give disguised instruction in the art of mental influence. Nearly every large concern employing selling agents has private instructors for their staff, who teach them the principles of mental influence disguised under the name of "Psychology of Business," or some such name.

And besides these, there are a number of people who have studied at the feet of some of the great metaphysical, semi-religious cults of the day, who have received instruction in mental influence disguised under the name of some creed or religious teachings, who have departed from the moral principles inculcated by their by their teachers, and who are using their knowledge in the shape of "treatments" of other persons for the purpose of influencing them to accede to their wishes or to act so as to bring financial gain to the person giving the treatment. There is self-protection possible to all, and this book will teach you how to use it.

Key Points

Under one name or another—under one form or another—mental influence has been operated and used from the earliest times. And today, even in the most remote portions of the globe, and among the most primitive and barbarous races peoples we find instances of the employment of this force.

Mental Influence is a great natural force, just as is electricity or any other natural forces, and it may be, and is, used for both good and evil purposes.

Mental Influence in itself is neither good nor bad. It is the individual who employs it who may be "good" or "bad," according to how it is used. The merit or demerit lies in the intention and purpose of the user, not in the force or power employed.

We have all felt ourselves, at some time or another in our lives, in the presence of individuals who almost compelled us to do what we knew in our hearts we should not do. Knowledge of the laws of mental influence would have enabled us to overcome the temptation.

CHAPTER 11

MAGIC—BLACK AND WHITE

The use of the word "magic" in connection with mental influence is quite ancient. Occultists make a clear distinction between the use of mental influence in a manner conducive to the welfare of others, and its use in a selfish, base manner calculated to work harm on others. Both forms are common and are frequently mentioned in all occult writings.

White magic has many forms, both in its ancient manifestations and in these latter days of revived occult knowledge. The use of mental influence in this way generally takes the form of kindly treatments of persons by others having their welfare at heart. In this particular class fall the various treatments of the several cults and schools of what is known as mental science, or similar names. These people make a practice of giving treatments, both "present" and "absent," for the purpose of healing physical ailments and bringing about a normal physical condition of health and strength. Similar treatments are given by some to bring about a condition of success to others, by imparting to the minds of such persons the vibrations of courage, confidence, energy, etc., which surely make for success along the lines of material occupation, etc.

In the same way one may treat adverse conditions surrounding others, bringing the force of the mind and will to bear on these conditions with the idea of changing the prevailing vibrations and bringing harmony from in-harmony, and success from failure.

The majority of persons, not informed along these lines, are surrounded by a mental atmosphere arising from the prevailing mental states, thoughts, feelings, etc., and also arising from the thought-currents which they have attracted to them by the *law of mental attraction*. These mental atmospheres, when once firmly settled around people, render it most difficult for them to "break away" from their vibrations. They struggle and fight, but the prevailing vibrations are beating down upon them all the time and must produce a strong effect upon even persons of strong will, unless indeed they have fully acquainted themselves with the laws of mental influence and have acquired the power of concentration. The habit of a lifetime, perhaps, has to be overcome, and besides the constant suggestive vibrations from the mental atmosphere are constantly bringing a pressure to bear upon these people, so that indeed they have a mighty task before them to throw off the old conditions, unaided and alone. And, so, while individual effort is preferable, there comes a time in the lives of many people when "a helping hand," or rather a "helping mind," is of great service and aid.

The person coming to the mental aid of people needing his or her services is performing a most worthy and proper act. We hear a great deal about "interfering with other people's minds" in such kind and worthy treatments, but in many cases there is but little real interference done. The work of the helper is really neutralizing and dissipating the unfavorable mental influences surrounding the people seeking help, and thereby giving these people a chance to work out their own mental salvation. It is true that everyone must do his or her own work, but help of the kind above indicated is surely most worthy and proper.

In these white magic treatments the person giving the treatments (the helper) forms the mental picture of the desired condition in his or her mind, and then sends thought-currents to the other person endeavoring to reproduce the mental picture in the mind or thought-atmosphere of that person. The best way of doing this, of course, is to assert mentally that the desired condition actually exists. One may be of great help and aid to others in this way, and there is no good reason why it should not be done.

The reverse side of this is a hateful form and manifestation of mental influence and many writers feel uncomfortable writing about it, but ignorance is no protection, and it is useless and foolish to pursue the policy of the ostrich which sticks its head in the sand when pursued, that not seeing the hunter the latter may not see him. It is better to look things in the face, particularly where it is a case of "forewarned being forearmed."

It is a fact known to all students of occultism that *black magic* has been frequently employed in all times to further the selfish, base aims of some people. And it is also known to advanced thinkers today that even in this enlightened age there are many who do not scruple to stoop to the use of this hateful practice in order to serve their own ends, notwithstanding the punishment that occultists know awaits such persons.

The annals of history are full of records of various forms of witchcraft, conjuration and similar forms of black magic. All the much talked of forms of "putting spells" upon people are really forms of black magic, heightened by the fear and superstition of those affected.

One has but to read the history of witchcraft to see that there was undoubtedly some force at work behind all of the appalling superstition and ignorance shown by the people of those times. What they attributed to the influence of people "in league with the devil" really arose from the use of black magic, or an unworthy use of mental influence, the two things being one. An examination of the methods used by these "witches," as shown by their confessions, gives us a key to the mystery. These "witches" would fix their minds upon other people, or their animals, and by holding a concentrated mental picture there, would send forth thought-waves affecting the welfare of the persons being "adversely treated," which would influence and disturb them, and often bring on sicknesses. Of course, the effect of these treatments were greatly heightened by the extreme ignorant fear and superstition held by the masses of people at the time, for fear is ever a weakening factor in mental influence, and the superstitions and credulity of the people caused their minds to vibrate in such a manner as to render them extremely passive to the adverse influences being directed against them.

It is well known that the Voodoos of Africa and Haiti, and similar cults practice black magic among their people with great effect. Among the natives of Hawaii there are certain men known as "Kahunas," who pray people sick, or well, whichever way they are paid for. There are other similar practices found all over the world.

In our own civilized lands there are many people who have learned the principles of mental influence, and who are using the same for unworthy purposes, seeking to injure others and defeat their undertakings, or else trying to bring them around to their own point of view and inclinations.

The modern revival of occult knowledge has operated along two lines. On the one hand we see and hear of the mighty power for good mental influence is exerting among the people today, raising up the sick, strengthening the weak, putting courage into the despondent and making successes of failures. On the other hand there are people who take advantage of this mighty force of nature and prostitute it to their own hateful ends, without heeding the dictates of conscience or the teaching of religion or morality. These people are sowing a baleful wind that will result in their reaping a frightful whirlwind on the mental plane. They are bringing down upon themselves pain and misery in the future.

At this point we wish to utter a solemn warning to those who have been, or are tempted, to employ this mighty force for unworthy purposes. The laws of the mental plane are such that "as one sows so shall he reap." The mighty *law of attraction* acts with the accuracy of a machine, and those who seek to entangle others in a net of mental influence sooner or later are caught by their own snare. The black-magician is sure to be sucked down into the whirlpool of his or her own making, and will be dragged down to the lowest depths. There are people who may feel appalled at the mention of the existence and possibilities of Black Magic. We remind these people that *good* always overcomes *evil* on the mental plane. A good thought always has the power to neutralize the evil one, and a person whose mind is filled with love and faith may combat a multitude whose minds are filled with hate and evil. The tendency of all nature is upward and toward good. And those who would pull it back toward evil sets themselves against the law of spiritual evolution, and sooner or later fall victim to their folly.

Thought-waves find entrance only to those minds that are accustomed to think similar thoughts. Those who *think* hate may be affected by hate thoughts, while those whose mind is filled with faith and love are surrounded by a resistant armor which repels the invading waves, and causes them to be deflected, or else driven back to their senders. Bad thoughts, like chickens, come home to roost. Thoughts act like boomerangs in their tendency to return to their sender. To the poison of black magic, nature gives the antidote of right thinking.

Key Points

The majority of persons are surrounded by a mental atmosphere arising from the prevailing mental states, thoughts, feelings, etc., and also arising from the thought-currents which they have attracted to them by the law of mental attraction. They may be good or evil.

The work of the helper is really neutralizing and dissipating the unfavorable mental influences surrounding the people seeking help, and thereby giving these people a chance to work out their own mental salvation.

We see and hear of the mighty power for good mental influence is exerting among the people today, raising up the sick, strengthening the weak, putting courage into the despondent and making successes of failures. On the other hand there is the hateful selfishness and greed of unprincipled persons in taking advantage of this mighty force of nature and prostituting it to their own hateful ends.

Those who think hate may be affected by hate thoughts, while those whose mind is filled with faith and deflect invading waves or else driven back to their senders.

CHAPTER 12
SELF-PROTECTION

Readers of the preceding chapters will see the power of mental influence in its various phases of manifestation, and will recognize the possibility of the force being used to influence them. The question that will naturally arise in the mind of every student and investigator of this important subject, and which comes to all at sometime, is: "How may I protect myself from the use of this power against myself? How may I render myself immune from these influences which may be directed against me?"

You are far less liable to succumb to bad mental influence if you maintain a mental atmosphere of high vibration—that is keeping yourself surrounded by a thought atmosphere filled with vibrations of the highest kind of thoughts and free from thoughts and desire of a base, selfish character, which tends to attract similar thoughts. In this way you create a state of mental hygienic cleanliness that renders you immune from the "contagious thoughts of the selfish plane of desire." This should be remembered and taken advantage of by everyone, for just as physical cleanliness gives no congenial lodgment for the germs of disease, so mental cleanliness refuses to admit the mental microbes.

But there is a method far more efficacious than even the above-mentioned plan. And this method is really that employed by the experienced occultists, and the method and practice taught the initiates of the occult brotherhoods and lodges all over the world.

In the first place, without entering into a statement of the details of the high occult teachings, the basic principle of all such teaching and instruction is that within each of us, in the very center of the being of each individual—in the very heart of hearts of the immortal ego—is what occultists know as the *flame of the spirit*. This is what you recognize in consciousness as the "I am" consciousness—that consciousness of being that is far above the consciousness of personality. It is that consciousness which informs each individual, unmistakably, that he or she *is* actually an individual being. This consciousness comes to the individual by reason of that person's contact with the great *one life of the universe*—it is the point of contact between the *part* and the *all*.

And in this part of our consciousness, coupled with the sense of *being,* there resides a spark from the divine flame of life and power, which is called the *inner will*. Do not mistake us and confuse this with the so-called "will of personality," which is merely a desire, or else certain firmness, which often is little more than stubbornness. This *inner will* is real power, and when once recognized may be drawn upon as a source of unending and unfailing strength. The occult experts have developed the consciousness of this *inner power*, and use it freely. This is the result of years of practice, and correct living and thinking. But, still, each and every person may draw upon this source of strength within them to aid them in life and to repel the thought-vibrations of the lower plane.

This consciousness may be developed by a realization of its existence, and by a practice of bringing the idea in everyday consciousness, by thought, meditation and practice. The very fact of having called your attention to its existence has awakened within the mind of you who are reading these lines a new strength and sense of power. Think a moment and see whether you do not feel a dawning sense of strength within you that you have not realized so fully before this moment! A continued recognition in your everyday consciousness of this *something within* will develop your ability to manifest it. Particularly in an hour of need will it spring to your assistance, giving you a sense of a part of yourself crying out to you in words of encouragement: *"I am here! Be not afraid!"*

It is very difficult to give you this method in written or printed words, but if you will enter fully into a recognition of this inward power you will find yourself developing a new power of resisting outside influences that will astonish you.

When you come in contact with people who are seeking to influence you in any of the ways mentioned in the preceding chapters of this book, or in others ways, you will find yourself able to defy their mental attacks by simply remembering the strength imminent in your "I," aided by the statement (made silently to yourself): "I am an *immortal spirit*, using my *inner will*." With this mental attitude you may make the slightest mental effort in the direction of throwing out from your mind vibrations, which will scatter the adverse influences in all directions, and which, if persisted in, will cause the other person to become confused and anxious to let you alone.

With this consciousness held in mind, your mental command to another, "Let me alone—I cast off your influence by the power of my spirit," will act so strongly that you will be able to actually see the effect at once. If the other person is stubborn and determined to influence you by words of suggestion, coaxing, threatening, or similar methods, look him or her straight in the eyes, saying mentally "I defy you—my inner power casts off your influence." Try this the next time that anyone attempts to influence you either verbally or by thought-waves and see how strong and positive you will feel, and how the efforts of the other person will fail. This sounds simple, but the little secret is worth thousands of dollars to every individual who will put it into practice.

Above all, put out of your mind all fear of others persons. The feeling of fear prevents you from manifesting the power within you to its full extent. Cast out fear as unworthy and hurtful.

Not only the case of personal influence in the actual presence of the other person may be defeated in this way, but the same method will act equally as well in the matter of repelling the mental influence of others directed against you in the form of "absent treatments," etc. If you feel yourself inclining toward doing something which in your heart you feel that is not to your best interests, judged from a true standpoint, you may know that, consciously or unconsciously someone is seeking to influence you in this way. Then smile to yourself and make the statements mentioned above, or some similar one, and holding the power of the spirit within your "I" firmly in you mind, send out a mental command just as you would in the case of the actual presence of the person himself or herself.

You may also deny the influencing power out of existence by asserting mentally: "I *deny* your power to influence me—you have no such power over me—I am resting on my knowledge of spirit and its will within me—I deny your power out of existence." This form of denial may be used either in the case of absent influence or personal influence. The rule is the same in all cases.

In repelling these absent influences you will at once experience a feeling of relief and strength and will be able to smile at the defeated efforts of the other person. If you feel sufficiently broad and full of love for humankind, you may then "treat" the other person for his or her error, sending thoughts of love and knowledge with the idea of dispelling that person's ignorance and selfishness, and bringing him or her to a realization of the higher truths of life.

You will doubtless have many interesting experiences arising from thus repelling these attacks. In some cases you will find that the next time you meet the person in question he or she will appear confused and puzzled and ill at ease. In other cases the person will begin to manifest a new respect and regard for you, and disposed to aid you instead of trying to influence you. In other cases the person will still have the desire, and will endeavor to "argue" you into doing that which he or she has tried to influence you into doing by mental influence, but these efforts will fail and without effect, particularly if you project another dose of the assertion of the power of the spirit within you.

In the same way you should call upon your higher self for aid and strength when you feel yourself being affected by any of the great mental waves of feeling or emotion sweeping over the public mind, and which have a tendency to "stampede" people into adopting certain ideas, or of following certain leaders. In such case the assertion of the "I" within you will dissipate the influence around you, and you will find yourself standing in a center of Peace surrounded on all sides by the ocean of mental tumult and agitation which is sweeping over or circling around the place. In the same way you will be able to neutralize the unpleasant mental atmospheres of places, localities, houses, etc., and render yourself positive to and immune from the same.

What you have learned in this book is a recipe that may be used in any and every instance of the employment of mental influence. It may sound simple to you, but a little use of it will make you deem it the most important bit of practical knowledge you may possess.

Key Points

You are far less liable to succumb to bad mental if you surround yourself with a thought atmosphere filled the highest kind of thoughts and free from thoughts and desire of a base, selfish character.

There resides a spark from the divine flame of life and power, which is called the *inner will*, and when once recognized will be a source of unending and unfailing strength.

Put out of your mind all fear of others persons. Cast out fear as unworthy and hurtful.

Assertion of the "I" within you will dissipate the influence around you, and will neutralize unpleasant mental atmospheres and render you immune from the same.

CPSIA information can be obtained
at www.ICGtesting.com
Printed in the USA
JSHW011018031119
2235JS00003B/33